ENGLISH DEPARTMENT
INDIANA UNIVERSITY OF PENNSYLVANIA
INDIANA, PENNSYLVANIA 15701

UNOBTRUSIVE
COMMUNICATION

Essays in Psycholinguistics

Prof. Dr. JOOST A.M. MEERLOO

Associate Professor of Psychiatry, New York School of Psychiatry
Lecturer in Political Psychology, New School for Social Research

ASSEN 1964 - THE NETHERLANDS

VAN GORCUM LTD. - DR. H. J. PRAKKE & H. M. G. PRAKKE

Printed in the Netherlands by Royal VanGorcum Ltd., Assen

This book is dedicated to my wife who not only collaborated in the linguistic part of it but also is a daily inspiration to explore the delights of communication

Foreword

A collection of essays written in different periods and read for different audiences is only then justified when they are pointed at an important common problem. The common denominator in these essays on psycholinguistics is the hidden exchange of feelings and thoughts between people.

My selection shows the way the word laboratory of the psychotherapeutic encounter gradually stimulated deeper interest into the total process of human communication. It starts with the intricate peculiarities of free association as applied in psychoanalytic technique and then expands to various Social interactions. The author is aware that although some of the chapters overlap each other they are each viewed from a different angle.

The practical implications of unobtrusive communication is enormous. In the cold war and in psychological warfare inadvertent suggestion is continually made use of.

Propaganda and advertising usually penetrate the mind without adaequate awareness of the recipient. The web of electronic communication is daily active in our living room; enough reason to emphasize this new network of human interactions.

JOOST A. M. MEERLOO

Contents

1. Psychoanalysis as an Experiment in Communication

The communication between patient and therapist may be viewed as a mere means to the goal of cure, giving insight to the manifold dynamics of therapy. Or, it may become itself an object of study – a fascinating world of uncharted dimensions of contact between man and his fellow man. In this laboratory of communication verbal and non-verbal forms of transmission play a role.

FREE ASSOCIATION AS A LINGUISTIC EXPERIMENT

In psychoanalytic treatment the method of free association, introduced by Freud, proves to be one of the best tools of self-revelation and deeper communication. The analysand is asked to forsake the realm of conventional, rational talk and thought and to reveal everything that is in his mind, without reserve. The therapist wants him to do this in order to arrive at the hidden primary process of unconscious feeling and thinking. The patient is not *pressed* to reveal all that comes to mind, but is gradually helped to feel free to voice and say anything and everything, unconditionally.

Very soon, however, it appears that this exercise in freely verbalizing all that enters the sphere of consciousness is rendered difficult by barriers of inner censorship. Usually there is less censorship if the therapist is able to prolong the first interview to three or four hours. We used this initial catharsis – the so called three-hour interview – in cases of war-neuroses, where no other form of treatment or second encounter with the patient were feasible.

What originally was called 'free' association appears to be not at all free; it is bound to numerous limitations and is modified in various ways. The flow of 'free association' is hampered by an infinite combination of feelings of shame, guilt, fear and hostile attitudes and unique inhibiting factors usually combined under the name resistance. The therapist plays an immediate role in the patient's form of censorship, even though apparently 'everything' may be said. The initial rapport and transference determines what the patient dares to say.

In subsequent sessions the 'free associations' reveal various modes of speech and communication, much as if the therapist were functioning in a speech laboratory.

This study is especially devoted to experiences in such verbal and non-verbal communications. The therapeutic situation is viewed as a laboratory for the study of microlinguistics. It is amazing to observe how many inner psychic processes go on during one therapeutic hour. Not only in words, but in silence – and silence can be just as informing as a maniacal revelation.

When we ask the patient to express without restraint what he is feeling and thinking, he often begins with a well-coordinated story, a report. He concentrates on central ideas and cannot verbalize the partial impressions that move at the periphery of his attention. He wants to communicate, to reveal, to conceal, to convince the therapist and himself. He cares too much about literal meaning. Only when he accepts and gradually realizes the revealing technique of free association will he turn inward, abandon conscious control of form, content, and direction of his words, and allow the stream of feelings and words to flow where it will. We may say that when a neurotic patient is really able to associate freely (in the psychoanalytic sense) he is, in effect, cured. The revelation of hidden meanings in free-flowing words and phrases occurs in various ways, in different tones and rhythms and at different levels of self-awareness. It is part of a normal process employed in meditative pondering and musing and it happens to everybody while listening to lectures or music. Psychoanalysis asks only that people think and communicate their ponderings aloud.

Here, however, a difficulty begins. When patients talk continuously and coherently in the therapeutic session, they rarely associate freely. If they use the 'grasshopper' technique, jumping from thought to thought, repressed ideas are more likely to come to the fore, with or without the analysand's conscious recognition of their significance. Sometimes a patient may talk only on the ego level, mouthing desultory, factual and sophisticated phrases; or his super-ego dams up the stream of spontaneous verbal production by compelling guilt-laden silence, morbid self-accusations, or moralistic diatribes. If there is little variation in the tone of his expression we may deduce a strong resistance to self-revelation. Often we recognize the various psychic 'levels' the patient expresses by tonal differences in his communication. Sometimes the musical tone is gone and the voice sounds mechanical; often the whining chant of the pouting, self-pitying child comes to the fore.

Many analysands use words merely to fill what is, to them, the terrifying, empty quiet of the therapeutic hour. They justify these short periods of silence by saying they are 'thinking.' But thinking, in this setting, usually indicates selection and the suppression of disturbing feelings and thoughts. All manner of speech habits are employed to escape the danger of self-revelation. Stuttering, stammering, 'sloganizing,' boasting, whining, scolding, the using of catch-words and truisms are all resorted to. In the motor and gestural area, rhythmic stroking, plucking, picking and scratching, chronic rigidity, restless tossing, or sudden changes of position may likewise substitute for the verbalization of ideas and feelings. In deep regression infantile rhythmic movements can be observed.

What we normally mean by the process of 'free association' comprises a duality of functions. The analysand is asked to focus on a certain content of his mind in order to communicate to the analyst, but at the same time to pay attention to what may jump

13

to mind besides. It is a simultaneous focusing and non-focusing. During therapy we often need to remind patients of this duality of attention.

Any form of expression, from loquacity to silence, from extensive gestural movement to frozen rigidity, may be indicative of resistance at some level of functioning. Following Spinoza's principle: *Omne determinatio est negatio* – every definition is a negation and limitation – we can make use of man's reluctance to express, to study his approximations of communication, his variations in *not* saying what he wishes or intends to say.

Beside the epistomological reason there exists an anthropological incentive; that of using the resistance to free association as a basis for linguistic study. In the ontogenetic process of man's humanization, his 'no,' his denial and frustration, take an important place. Man is the animal that can say 'no' to his instinctual drives. He does not automatically have to yield to his biological adaptation. Man's linguistic detour, his speech and creativity are related to this process of taking distance from instinctual drives. In our clinically descriptive study, it is not necessary to trace the origin of man's verbal communication. This has been done with great skill by Spitz[12] in his recent book, *No and Yes.*

Neurosis compels the patient to behave, in therapy, like an army in strategic withdrawal, giving ground only when a new defensive position has been selected. Preferably a hideout is sought from which a counter-offensive can be launched. Therefore, to speak merely of 'eliminating' or 'dissolving' resistance, as many therapists tend to do, is unrealistic, for all life patterns – and especially man's magic attempt to eternalize himself through the verbalization of thoughts – are resistances against more deeply hidden fears of death and the unknown. Equally unrealistic is the belief, implicit in some forms of psychotherapy, that unlimited free flow of recall and the consequent connection of past experiences with the present *per se*, will effect a positive reorganization of the psyche. Some patients with defective ego-structure use such unlimited verbiage and revelation in order to resist growing up and becoming a mature person with reserve and composure.

Even among psychoanalysts one frequently finds the idea (expressed or implied) that timely questions, leads and interpretations of the resistance by the analyst are the best means of 'overcoming' inner defenses and stimulating the free flow of associations, and that patient adherence to this technique produces the most positive results in conquering the resistance in the service of cure. More often it is the hidden 'free association' and the shock-like, sudden intuitive comprehension of the analyst – his own 'Aha' experience – followed by interruption and a new interpretation, that breaks through the prolonged resistance of the patient. Though, in the course of the therapeutic process the latter may have entered a phase of verbalizing confusion without clarification, with good rapport and transference, the new revelation may undo the defensive maneuver.

Let us re-examine the therapeutic instrument of free verbalization and introduce several technical considerations which may help to clarify the internal dynamics and dialectics of the therapeutic communication and thereby facilitate a more comprehensive view of the total process.

I shall begin by summarizing the chief ways in which 'free' association is employed as various modes of resistance by patients:

1. It may be used selectively, as spokesman for one mental system and to the exclusion of the others; for the ego (most common in character neurosis), for the super-ego (as in obsession-compulsion neurosis) or for the id (as in psychopathy and borderline cases).

2. It may be used selectively in a temporal sense; for example, the patient may free-associate chiefly about the present, excluding allusions to the past, or vice versa.

3. It may be used as a verbal disguise to suppress or repress affect-anxiety, guilt, aggression or sexual excitement arising from silence.

15

4. It may be used to ward off emotions, physical sensations and motoric impulses.
5. It may be used as a direct instrument of transference; to eliminate the analyst with verbal noises (symbolically: kill off), or to attract him with minute musical clues and verbal tentacles (symbolically: seduce him). Talking replaces non-verbalized feeling here. The therapist is drowned in mumbo-jumbo.

That these underlying motivations are altogether clear to the therapist as far as level and content of inner verbalized material are concerned, is of less importance than the fact that certain patients may, for long periods, remain unaware of these motivations and also impervious to the therapist's interpretation of the resistance factors at work. This type of patient free-associates to the best of his ability, saying many things that come into his mind but unconsciously repressing many others. He is singularly unable to recognize the disguised selective nature of his 'free' associations, especially when his verbalizations are affectively charged. Such loquacious cases may go on for years without substantial improvement[10] when the underlying primary excretory meaning of this form of free association is not sufficiently worked through.

PATTERNS OF FREE ASSOCIATION

The following observations reveal more about the manifold speech habits used as verbal cues and verbal pitfalls where free association is used in the service of resistance rather than for direct expression. Certainly, many more patterns could be mentioned and some of the patterns described here overlap each other!

1. *Actualization:* Free association about actual occurrences only; the past is never touched.
2. *Noncommittal talk:* Careful, uninvolved, selected topics.
3. *Filling time:* Free association as babble and prattle, to gain

time against the real confession;· saying something to delay saying something else.

4. *Verbal delay:* Free association only towards the end of the hour. The patient, after stalling and marking time, submits temporarily to the procedure, only to prevent the trauma of departure or to make good for wasted time. Direct explanation of this ambivalent speech habit is often very helpful.

5. *Escape into dream analysis:* The patient chooses only to talk about dreams, preferring the magic of dream symbolism and taking the dream as a guide in order to remain in his infantile magic world. He often announces the dream in a chanting way. This strategy is frequently seen in borderline cases and often comprises a subtle testing of – and jeering at – the therapist.

6. *Ritualization of the stream of words:* Free association has in itself become a ritual. There is a compulsion to be objective and logical, with perfect intellectual control of expressions.

7. *Jocular defense:* Punning, joking, and many slips of the tongue, all serving to deny infantile material.

8. *Sloganizing:* Rigid speech habits are displayed, word crutches, clichés, repetitions, euphemisms, interjections [1] useful elsewhere for purposes of disguise.

9. *'Nonsensification':* Senseless associations are concocted as a strategy of confusion, especially by compulsives. As with all their symptoms, they overshoot the mark, defying their parental training and the analytic rule.

10. *Verbal crutching:* Free association is used to flee from silence (the latter often representing reminiscences of the primal scene). There is talking, with automatic word clichés, instead of thinking and awareness.

11. *Verbal tantalizing:* The analyst is pinned down by words, any word. Talking is used as an aggressive, sneering challenge.

12. *Verbal seduction:* Talking is a quest for love. Words are used as erotic tentacles. Talking is designed to provoke the analyst to talk to and love the patient. He (or she) waits with uncanny empathy and identification for the emotion he may arouse in the therapist.

17

13. *Aggressive word diarrhea:* The patient uses free association as an ancient magic defiance of any control. The patient lets fly words in order to soil, to defy or to bite back. He wants only to discuss something as a substitute for (anal) aggression. This phenomenon is often encountered in compulsives and they are frequently aware of the intention of such loquacity.

14. *Word incontinence:* A manic attitude is displayed and the patient doesn't focus at all. (Logorrhea: a diarrhea of words without awareness.) No centralizing factor in the ego directs the communication from person to person.

15. *Verbal constipation:* The pressure of thinking hard and keeping in: When the patient thinks, he usually selects and he does not want to express.

16. *Gestural pathos:* Theatrical gestures are employed as a defense against talking.

17. *Camouflage:* The skin plays a dual role of *expression* and *camouflage of emotions* (as I will show in the next chapter). This is a reversion to archaic mimicry.

18. *Organ language:* In the use of organ language we see the remnants of early conversions and psychosomatic conditioning. Among these psychosomatic defenses, pains, aches and the common cold play a most important role.

19. *Over-defensive self-accusation:* Talking is used as masochistic self-accusation and false confession and shows the wish for punishment.

20. *Pouting and crying:* In incessant crying we see the strategy of self-pity used over and over, as uncontrolled complaining and the collecting of injustices. Crying may also be used to ward off deeper guilt about seeing and peeping (primal scene).

21. *Vertiginous verbiage:* When dizziness accompanies the fear of free association it means that dangerous thoughts and reminiscences still remain suppressed. It often represents awareness of suicidal feelings or early sensations of falling with the infantile reminiscence of utter insecurity. The patient talks himself into a tizzy.

22. *Polarity verbiage:* People may use words to unobtrusively hide the semantic counterpart of the ambivalence, meaning

the opposite. They say, 'I love you,' but mean, 'I hate you, I want to devour you.' By now we know that every word has an ambiguous, equivocal meaning. Etymology provides many examples of the opposite meanings hidden in words. The French word *Sacré* means blessed and cursed. Cold, *kalt, caldo, chaud* (warm) are the same word. Host and hostile have the same linguistic root. The word 'taboo' means 'holy' but also 'unclean.' Freud showed that through slips of the tongue a meaning, opposite to the meaning consciously intended, often breaks through man's barrier of politeness.

23. *Paradoxical clarity:* When the patient talks too clearly the pressure of keeping in secrets is evident. As the Chinese used to say, 'Those who talk about Tao, don't know Tao.'

24. *Cold objectivity:* A total lack of transference and rapport, disguised by cold objectivity, is usually a defense against libidinal and aggressive drives. In many cases the patient's knowledge of the theory of analysis spoils his ability to associate freely. He escapes into over-intellectualization and constantly tries to drag the therapist into a sophisticated conversation. The resulting therapeutic silence is typically felt as unbearable by both parties.

PATTERNS OF SILENCE

The strategy of silence and silent denial is a well-known defense mechanism. However, in recent years, more attention has been given to this word-denying strategy, which is so often used by patients when they should be talking.[2] The dual nature of silence as a means of expression and camouflage becomes apparent.

Among children and primitive peoples, the strategy of silence is deliberately exploited to excommunicate and annihilate the enemy symbolically or to ward off some other threatening danger. Here silence serves either as a sort of ostrich policy or a magical excommunication of angry ghosts. 'Don't talk about them – don't tempt fate by speaking of them...' The Mayas had a god of silence, who was a very hostile god.

In conversation and discussion, silent non-conformism is often experienced as more hateful than overt verbal aggression.

In psychoanalytic treatment, too, patients use silence primarily as resistance to – or revenge against – the analyst. Most people feel the vacuum of silence to be a sinister threat. Children, especially, fear the parent who punishes with silence and with the gaze of the evil eye. For them such fascination and be-witchment means magic annihilation. In England, fascination with the evil eye is still a legally punishable act.

Threatening emotional experiences force people to become silent, for verbal expression proves inadequate. The stress of war and battle makes many a soldier mute. Or people remain silent be-cause they fear sounding trivial.

In normal conversation, even in scientific discussion, there also exists a fear of silence. Once it occurs, a contagious feeling of discomfort and tension are evoked. ('Words are sometimes only spoken to break the tension of silence, or to evade the conspiracy of silence.' – H.G.Wells.) But there also exists a communion of silence, the veneration of silence as a binding force, the ecstasy of silence, representing the wordless contact between mother and child. The Quaker meeting uses silent meditation as a means of increased communion; so do many oriental rituals. One of my borderline patients clung six months to his strategy of silence, than thanked me for not having intruded into his meditations; and from then on he cooperated. Silence may be pure hostility and resistance toward revealing hidden guilt or sexual wishes. However, the patient is most often silent becanse he is thinking aggressively or sexually about the therapist.[3]

Fliess [2] published an excellent study on the intricate relations be-tween silence and verbalization. I condense his and my own experiences in the following scheme. Silence may represent:

1. *Physiological inhibition*: Limited speech is the result of arrested psychosomatic development. Affective confusion. [4] Con-ditioned aphasia or mutism.

2. *Reminiscence of the silence of the womb:* The silence represents vague meditations on death and eternity or a regression to intrauterine fantasies. We like to call it pre-verbal communication.

3. *Oral erotic silence:* The silent ecstasy of deep oral gratification inhibits speech. Sexual secrecy of infantile experiences may cut off communication. The speechless peeping infant may have been caught in an ambivalent awe and terror.

4. *Urethral-erotic silence:* Silence means symbolic stoppage of the stream of words and the gift of body fluids. The primary struggle with toilet habits is displaced toward sobbing, gasping and crying. The patient wants help in cleaning himself from dirty words.

5. *Anal erotic silence:* Silence here means verbal constipation; keeping words, thoughts and body-products stubbornly in. Tenseness is expressed in rubbing the head or other parts of the body. A constant struggle against verbalization goes on. The denial of words represents the refusal to give body and mind content, undifferentiated by the young child.

6. *Genital silence:* Silence represents taboo against the expression of a direct sexual wish. It represents the fear of the promiscuity of words, for every word is sexualized. The silence covers up guilt, anxiety, shame, but the patient can also experience the pleasant promiscuity of silent fantasy. As long as nothing is said there is no taboo.

7. *Transference silence:* The analyst represents the parent who did not furnish the required words of information. Through silence, the patient provokes the repetition of an old tragedy: the lost love of the parents who did not give words of affection.

8. *Silence as repressed aggression:* Speaking is a trial act; yet words may kill. Silence represents the fear of attacking with words or its opposite, the fear of being verbally attacked by the therapist.

The Nazis officially recognized and tortured the silent nonconformists among their prisoners. The stubbornness they purported to read on their prisoners' silent faces was called 'physiognomical insubordination.' Prisoners in their strategy of non-cooperation were not allowed silent protest; they had to look stupidly meek and innocent, otherwise the aggressor feared the silent reproach of his victim. In the process of brainwashing remaining silent was also the greatest crime.

'Speech is silver but silence is golden.' To be able to safeguard secrets is proof of mental strength and discipline. Secret knowledge is only accorded those initiates who know the value of silence. The technique of free association is in conflict with the conditioned silence that prevails in certain cultures and communities.

Some monastic orders require their members to maintain complete silence on the wisdom that thoughtless and light-minded talk damages the soul. St. Benedict imposed this rule on his order after the opening of Monte Casino. *Mors et vita in manibus linguae*, says the rule of the Benedictines – 'Death and life lie in the hands of the tongue.' Since almost superhuman effort is needed to maintain absolute silence, a complicated gesture language has developed in several monasteries, though even gesture language is regarded by some members of the order as immoral.

The silence related to understanding deeper than speech, as revealed in the eternal symbols of art, may be called the revelation of the creative unconscious.[11] The unconscious is honest and naked in its aims. In one moment of unmasking, man may see and know a glimpse of ecstatic insight or intuition that knows no words; silence and empathy unite him in his feelings with the essence of all things, as the infant was magically united with the world in his preanimistic feeling. The Orientals, especially, have cultivated the ceremonial of being together in silence and meditation. The modern Western writer tries to indicate in his dialogues what is also unspoken between men. In literary art we not only read the reality and semantics of the printed words, but also that which goes far beyond. Rhythmic style and redundant silence play just as much a communicative role as the words themselves.

In the therapeutic situation, the silent, unconscious, pre-verbal pattern of exchange that may gradually develop, can be detected in changes of gesture and timbre of the sounds. To understand the meaning of those silences is part of the skill and art of therapy; they, too, have to be verbalized gradually.

Experiences occur apart from word and speech. Our common word-images are masks sold in the market place. However, the patient in his attempt to conquer repressed material has to verbalize what is often inexpressible in common words. This is one of the perennial linguistic dilemmas of the therapeutic process.

PATTERNS OF CONFESSION

The better we understand the paradoxical motivations behind people's urge to talk about themselves, the better we shall understand the chaotic ways of speech and communication of the talking patient. True, talking unburdens the heart and frees the mind, and to express oneself is to redeem oneself. But this is only the conscious part of it; unconsciously, the opposite urge to hide behind so-called confession may be much greater.

Trace any conversation, and you will see that ultimately it leads to some form of unobtrusive confession or disguise. Normal conversation is a kind of communal free association. More intense catharsis may take place in people who find the right person to 'talk it out' to. Through their personalities, some invite others to express themselves. I have often noted that ego-weak compulsive patients with an uncanny gift of identifying with others induce verbal intimacies in others. It is as though a special magical influence emanates from them to arouse feelings of confidence and trust. They respond to a universal transference need,[6] and the confessants feel that all their confidences are safe. Under special circumstances the urge to communicate and to confess can be self-destructive. Prisoners in the hands of inquisitors and brainwashers can be so tempted to communicate and talk to someone in their loneliness, that they finally confess more crimes than they have actually committed.

General confession to friends or to one's religious advisor – has

23

an important function in the communion of words. But a psychological dilemma arises in each such cathartic conversation. People both like and dislike talking. Really painful things cannot be told. Whatever is confessed is usually a defense against deeper (unknown) guilt. I regard skeptically all those who speak with the pathos of seemingly open truth and honesty; behind this tactic there often lies the most perfidious form of hypocrisy, for much confession is pure strategy to provoke someone else's deeper secrets in exchange for superficial ones.

The following survey elaborates the psychological patterns and pitfalls of confession. In the free-associating patient confession may mean:

1. *Seduction:* Words are used as erotic currency; telling secrets seeks to induce counter-secrets. Confession may also be intended to provoke the sexual promiscuity of mutual remorse: 'How bad I am, but love me nevertheless.' Verbal exhibitionism and verbal incontinence are often used as sexual invitation or as infantile anal magic to ensnare the therapist. 'When I use obscene words to you I am already taking magic possession of you.'

2. *Boasting:* 'Please admire my inner complications, my guilt and my crimes.'

3. *Covering up:* Confession of lesser crimes serves to hide deeper ones (confession compulsion as a defense). It may also displace what should be confessed elsewhere. (Parent, police, church.)

4. *Doing and undoing:* Ambivalence; only one side of the coin is shown. Confession permits undoing of the guilt and implicitly grants the right to start all over again. Confession substitutes for action to remedy the crime or mistake.

5. *Catharsis:* Confession is made to get rid of dirt, guilt, shame and hostility. As with anal aggression and anal magic, the confessor henceforth carries the responsibility. The confession can also be used to slander other participants in the 'plot.'

6. *Confession as a paradoxical defense against the urge to ask taboo*

questions: Primal scene reminiscences compel persons to confess and to ask new questions.

7. *Wish for love:* 'I want to confess in order to become worthy of you.'

8. *Wish for punishment and absolution:* Confession as religious duty (confession to the representative of the moral order).[9] Catharsis occurs through the sacrament of penance and remorse. The confession can be motivated by the wish to correct oneself and to grow out of infantile patterns of behavior. Again, there exists a masochistic enjoyment throug self-accusation; the search for punishment can become a secondary defense against deeper-seated neurotic guilt.

Personal confession may also have a liberating effect outside the treatment situation because people feel that their words are safe with close confidants. With them they can free themselves of the spasmodically-retained gesture, of the fear and guilt connected with repressed and disturbing ideas. Yet, they already experience great redemption – which precedes all verbal confession – in the awareness that there is a silent listener to whom they can confess even in the silent communion of the therapeutic hour. The therapist is temporarily the image of the all-knowing, forgiving parent. Without working through parental conflicts genuine confession is impossible.

Psychoanalysis does not replace religious confession, but prepares those who feel too frustrated, hesitant or reluctant, to exercise their own moral prerogatives.

PATTERNS OF SPEECH FUNCTION

The technique of free association and free verbalization throws a special light on speech habits and on what transpires behind normal conversation and communication. Just because the daily therapeutic experience is a grotesque caricature of normal speech, the technique of free association informs us of the various functions included in speech and communication far exceeding linguistic experiences. The analytic situation has taught us how

25

varied are the means of communication that man uses: pre-verbal, gestural, sound, organ-language and finally his verbal patterns. Precise language is more often used as inhibition of free rapport than as communication: *People only understand each other through the use of several types of communicative functions.* The combination and integration of these functions helps to overcome the semantic limitation of the static word.

A final summary presents the different aims of speech and verbal communication as it is found in the daily word-laboratory of psychoanalytic therapy. Verbal communication represents:

1. *The need to express*, to give vent to emotions and moods, the need to signal. Such speech has the same biologic signal function as that of animals. The word is a shout, a cry for help, a warning, a defiance, an infantile discharge of affect.

2. *The need to make sounds;* lust for noise (Schwatzbedürfniss), onomatopeia. The word is escape from silence. Words and noises ward off anxiety. The word is pure motoric release. Sound has become magic defense against the unknown. The word is mere play; playing with the mouth.

3. *The need for contact*, for human companionship. The desire to conform, to be cozy. The word bridges inter-human space. Talking and fantasying are used in the service of giving and gaining attention.

4. *The need to communicate*, to inform, to state facts. Word becomes a semantic sign. This is particularly the rhetorical and persuasive function of language.

5. *The need to create*, to formulate ideas, to produce. Speech is used as a trial, a transitional act preceding the overt act.

6. *The need to confront the world.* The word becomes a means of aggression, or the beginning of scientific curiosity. Illusions, hope and white lies can be produced, yet the word has become a means of separation from reality.

7. *The need for individuation*, self-assertion and awareness of existence, the need to 'distantiate' from others and from one's own emotions. The word has become a means of confronting reality. 'I want to give reality its own proper name.'

8. *The need to control*, as exercised by the magic gestures of children and primitive peoples, who name things in order to possess them magically. This magic function of the word we find especially expressed in compulsive behavior. The word has become a tool of magic strategy in the service of omnipotence.

9. *The need to control others* or to be controlled by them. The need to be the center of attention. This strategy may be expressed verbally in: *a.* Attempts to evoke word-or-deed reaction in the listener, the need to induce his cooperation. *b.* direct command; *c.* assertion of opinion; *d.* withholding of words; reservation of opinion; *e.* direct magic strategy – naming of things and persons to reduce their mysterious and hence threatening aspects – vilification, cold war, verbal strategy; cursing, excommunication.

10. *Sexual desire;* the word searches for the willing partner through the guiltless promiscuity of words. The word is flirtation, anticipation, a sexual tentacle.

11. *The word serves as camouflage and defense mechanism.* The need to deceive, disguise, to use utter falsehoods. The need to conceal thought or the absence of thought. The need to confuse others. Subtle mannerisms of communication have become part of disguising character defenses. Word-crutches and neologisms are used as concealment. Talking is used to cover up guilt and shame.

12. *The need to inadvertently express unconscious motives* through slips of the tongue, through stammering, lapses, mistakes, tics, rituals, witticisms and obscure terminology. Speech becomes a compulsive repetition of mumbo-jumbo in the service of frustrated drives.

13. *The refusal of contact*, as we see in psychotic negativism and neurotic inhibition of speech.

REFERENCES

1. FELDMAN, S.S., Mannerisms of Speech. *Psychoanalytic Quarterly*, Vol. 17, 1948.
2. FLIESS, R., Silence and Verbalization. *International Journal of Psychoanalysis*, Vol. 30, 1949.
3. FREUD, S., *Psychopathology of Everyday Life*. New York: Modern Library, 1938.
4. LURIA, A.R., *The Nature of Human Conflicts*. New York: Liveright, 1932.
5. MEERLOO, J.A.M., *Delusion and Mass Delusion*. New York: Nervous and Mental Disease Monographs, 1949.
6. MEERLOO, J.A.M., and M.L. COLEMAN: The Transference Function. *Psychoanalytic Review*, Vol. 38, 1951.
7. MEERLOO, J.A.M., Telepathy as a Form of Archaic Communication. *Psychiatric Quarterly*, Vol. 23, 1949.
8. MEERLOO, J.A.M., *Communication and Conversation*. New York: International Universities Press, 1958 (2nd printing).
9. SHEEN, MONSIGNOR F.J., *Psychoanalysis and Confession*. Washington: Catholic University of America. 1951.
10. OBERNDORF, C.P., Unsatisfactory Results of Psychoanalytic Therapy. *Psychoanalytic Quarterly*, Vol. 29, 1950.
11. SACHS, H., *The Creative Unconscious*. Cambridge: Sci-Art Publishers, 1947.
12. SPITZ, R.A., *No and Yes*, On the Genesis of Human Communication. New York: International Universities Press. 1957.

2. Human Camouflage and Identification with the Environment

THE CONTAGIOUS EFFECT OF ARCHAIC SKIN SIGNS

THE USE OF ANALOGIES IN CLINICAL OBSERVATION

Camouflage and mimicry are biological defense mechanisms observed throughout the animal kingdom. The animal is able to change color and form in such a way that it will be inconspicuous to its enemies.

This need to be inconspicuous and unobserved is just as well known to man. Though he usually resorts to a behavioral strategy in order to become 'anonymous' and thus blend with his surroundings, in periods of great stress he may unwittingly resort to rudimentary remnants of biological defenses older than the more passive identification with and surrender to the enemy [5] which we observe in the human animal.

In 1931 I described a passive behavioral defense mechanism which I called the *passive surrender to danger*.[17] The person possessed by undifferentiated fear and anxiety, instead of fleeing from or fighting the danger, surrendered, blended, and collaborated with the dreaded instance. The criminal who lives in constant fear of being caught by the police prefers to give himself up in order to free himself from the tension of anticipation. Several examples of imitations of a passive catalepsy-like conduct were mentioned. People behaved as if hypnotized by danger. I observed this reaction predominantly in children, primitive people, and psychotics. Defensive camouflage was mentioned as

29

part of this passive strategy of surrender to the stronger party. In 1946, Anna Freud described in her book on ego defenses an analogous defensive strategy, which she called *identification with the aggressor*. It is the involuntary imitation of the feared person, the strategy of overcoming the anxiety of passive submission through more actively playing the role of the aggressor. [5] It is 'living by proxy,' identifying with the emotions of the feared person. Magic gestures and actions serve to convey that the person in panic knows himself to be dangerous and endangered at the same time.

Both human camouflage and human communication are rooted in the animal signals of communication. Originally these signals were used ambiguously, either as a means of warning and to convey a state of alarm to fellow creatures, or to hide or camouflage, exposing what the neurologist calls the mask and reflex of threat and grandeur.[10] This two-fold form of signaling, as a warning or a disguise, in reply to an external event is regarded by several linguists as a forerunner of our speech and verbal communication.[13]

The study of this phylogenetic old signal system – mostly controlled by the sympathetic, parasympathetic, and endocrinological system – is of importance because man's preverbal and presymbolic communication often makes use of these rudimentary biological signaling devices. In our verbal communication, and more so when we regress to a more primitive existence, we will frequently revert to some of these innate archaic patterns of communication as, for instance, mere excited sound production or uncoordinated gesture language.[12]

Of additional interest is the contagious effect of these biological signals. Mental infection and psychic mass contagion are for the greater part stimulated and transferred by the common regression to and empathy with these archaic means of expression.

The phenomena of camouflage and emotional expression can be studied from various angles, though in our phase of scientific development we have to limit ourselves mostly to clinical descriptions and psychological analogy and metaphor. The causal relations have to be proved by a more intensive, multidisciplinary exploration. Darwin, who was one of the first to write an elaborate book on the subject of the expression of emotions in man and animal, did this in a purely descriptive way.[4] Since Darwin much discussion developed around the assumption of homologous mechanisms for analogous behavior. One of the basic questions is: What did our sociocultural conditioning do to the appropriate biological patterns of behavior innate in man? The ethologist Tinbergen[27] reproaches the comparative psychologists that not enough attention is given to innate behavior (*ethology*, science of 'objective' behavior) and that a preoccupation exists about comparison with prehuman behavior. Yet, he finds with Parsons[7] the problem-solving device more important than the blind adherence to rigid methods.[26]* Schneirla warns against faulty anthropomorphism.[23]

The use of analogy and metaphor in our thinking is related to the so-oft-neglected historical method in clinical medicine, in which we regard every individual as a unique and incidental 'meeting point' of various causal rules.[16] In this legitimate ideographic and individual approach – which contrasts with the statistical and causal reductive approach – we identify unobtrusively with a purposeful constructor. The danger of this doctrine of ends and goals, however, is that we may project too much of our own purposive striving on the phenomena under investigation. But the opposite is also true. We may identify too much and mistakenly with some purposeless, statistical, and mechanical construct (a machine).[20] Analogy and metaphor

---

* Parsons: But, cannot the idea of recapitulation be applied, with many qualifications, to the relation between the development of socio-cultural systems historically, the origins of which are entirely obscure, and the development of the individual within such a system? Is not cultural evolution a chapter in biological evolution?

Emerson: We cannot predict from one level to the other, but since the biological and the socio-cultural levels show other parallels, they might well show these parallels also.

Parsons: This parallelism was assumed in a very schematic and naive way a generation or two ago. Then the evolutionary approach was discredited, but now I think we can approach the problem in a much more sophisticated way. *Toward a Unified Theory of Human Behavior*, pp. 209-11.[7]

teach us to see what has later to be verified with clinical data.

At the end of an over-all investigation the fallacies of mere causal and purely ideographic approaches should be integrated. Finding analogies is a clinical and convenient way of discovering relationships in coincidental similar constructs, the deeper sense of which has to be proved at a later date. The ideographic or historical method, however, brings us nearer to the fundamental reason or ultimate goals related to the event that took place.

Since separation and the severed motherchild symbiosis play an increasingly important role in human psychology, investigation of communication as a response to separation becomes more and more important. Simple biologic sign systems develop in the service of the expression of simple emotions like pain, rage, anger, fear, shame, disgust. They have a twofold meaning: on the one hand they are tokens of inner turmoil, of alarm and mobilization, on the other, they are a form of communication signaling warning to other beings. However, communication finds its highest expression in language and verbal creation.

FIRST ENCOUNTER: FEAR-MELANOSIS AND SYNCOPE

The first time the clinical problem of man reverting to archaic communication became real to me was when I was called to give medical first aid with a military outfit to bombed-out and ruined Rotterdam. We encountered neither overt panic nor anxiety reactions as described in the existing psychiatric literature. Instead, we found most of those people who had gone through days of burning hell strangely calm and mechanical in their reactions – in fact, too calm. Yet they had changed in a way we could hardly describe. Everybody looked older than he was, dried out, with a wrinkled face.

At first we thought that lack of water and the hot whirling dust of the holocaust could have caused these skin changes. But what we observed was a much more generalized skin syndrome. It afflicted even the people who had stayed in rather safe shelters with enough intake of food and fluids. In some people more definite dermatological complaints developed: urticaria, eczema, itching, profuse sweating. In addition they showed lack of appetite, frequent urination – with resulting disturbed sleep – and a generalized mental irritability. It was not until months later that some of the victims under my treatment developed typical anxiety reactions combined with lack of mental control – as if a certain incubation period were needed to bring out more serious mental trouble. It was during that period that several patients directed my attention to discolorations of the skin, hyper-pigmentated patches, which were to stay for a long time, and sudden graying of hair. A recent publication[2] doubts the sudden whitening of the hair, yet in those days I saw it happen myself. It may begin with the appearance of a few white streaks soon after which a general graying follows. Elsewhere in the litera-ture we find mentioned sudden alopecia, a complete loss of body hair as a reaction to sudden fright and panic.[8] I myself developed a form of fear-melanosis, a sudden brown patch on my forehead the day after (by good luck) I was able to escape sure death at the hands of the Nazis.

Search in the literature for references to these startling skin reactions did not reveal very much, only that during the First World War various cases of overpigmentation of the skin were described and explained as a result of severe mental stress suffer-ed by incessant gun barrage over a period of months in trench warfare.[22] This syndrome was then called *fear melanosis;* it was combined with various pathologic changes in the sympathetic innervation: edema, profuse sweating, increased irritability.

The observation of this peculiar skin activity in periods of extreme danger and stress directed the attention toward the psychophysiologic function of the skin not only as an organ of protection but also as a system of communication of various alarm signals towards the outside world.

Only much later did I understand why the people of bombed Rotterdam had so many skin eruptions, why they constantly yawned, why they behaved in such an imitative and mechanical cataleptic manner – as if trying to assume a vast camouflage, and through it a hiding from fate. Similar sign behavior, as for instance utter paleness, seen not only in acute fright or anger but also in various forms of regression, we experience in psychotic patients. We often see that it forces the psyche of sympathetic bystanders into the same kind of feelings of anxiety and regression as the victim is experiencing. We may see such empathy-provoking skin behavior in an increased measure in the stigmata of hysteria and, to relate another war experience, in contagious mass-fainting of soldiers standing at attention during inspection. It reminds us of the fact that vasodepressor syncope is not only a question of cerebral ischemia but also a symbolic response acting upon various unconscious fantasies and with far-reaching communicative implications.

THE PHYSIOLOGICAL IDENTIFICATION WITH THE ENVIRONMENT

How can we explain the empathy-provoking action of the skin? The skin is our first physical boundary as well as an organ of reception and defense in response to various stimuli from the outside world. It is the organ of communication between the inner and the outer world. Ontogenetically, the skin and our nervous system are derived from the same blastocystic ectodermal layer, and consequently the skin remains a part of our system of internal regulation.[1] We see its defensive function especially in lower animals, where manifold skin processes help the animal to camouflage itself or to threaten the attackers.[15, 25] Man, with his rudimentary skin functions, has in many ways perfected the use of his skin for self-display, for attraction, and for disguise.[12] However, man, the fetalized, dependent mammal, can no longer, as the many lower animals still can, encyst himself in a hardened skin,* or expand into a fearsome, threatening giant like a cat in

* Perhaps we are allowed to compare ichthyosis with this reactive formation of skin armor and fortified ectoderm. In 1952, the *British Medical Journal* dedicated an editorial to the importance of ectodermal adaptation to environment. In the same publication Mason describes a case of congenital ichthyosis *cured* by hypnosis (Brit. M. J., August 23, 1952), after grafting and other forms of plastic surgery had proved unsuccessful.

anger, nor can he produce the outer changes of color like the chameleon. Yet it is as if in extreme danger part of those rudimentary warning and alarm signals spring into life. The human skin, like that of horses, has its own rudimentary motoric defenses – the remnants of the platysma and the pylomotoric reflexes that cause our goose flesh. Our hair can stand on end, we may bristle with courage, and rudimentary attempts at protective coloration go into action.

In the womb the skin is not yet exposed, it rests in the warm amniotic fluid. There is no shivering and shuddering; no creeping feelings are felt. These begin at birth. Many subsequent shiver reactions – related to danger and fear – betray this initial archaic protection against exposure.[12]

With their emotional skin reactions human beings often experience subjectively that they are trying to communicate to others a threat, an alarm, or an appeal. The psychoanalytic session is the scene of reactivation of many such manifestations. In *anger* we flush with hatred and grow 'purple with rage' as if we wanted to jump out of our skins. Muscles and vessels are in tension, ready for the jump, and meanwhile we show our teeth, ready to bite. In *shyness* or in *shame* the hot blushing skin covers our nothingness, encompassing, as it were, our naked body. We find such reactions more persistent in patients suffering from rosacea. In *fear* we try to express the feeling of helplessness and lack of power; yet, while appealing for help, simultaneously we attempt to be more threatening. Our rudimentary skin defense tries to behave like the threatening fur of the cat. Cold sweat may break out and we become 'white with fear.' When disgusted we pull in our lips or show a sour face.[21]

In popular language archaic skin reactions also play a role. Unwittingly and unconsciously reminiscences of archaic reactions to danger are revealed in such popular sayings: 'Somebody is walking over one's grave,' when one shivers and gets goose pimples. Especially in sexual behavior many of those rudimentary signals may come back. We don't spread our feathers like the peacock, but his best tie and her nicest jewelry and perfume reminds us of the most festive and active animal

35

communications by means of colors, odors, and sounds during the rutting and copulation season.

Thanks to the development of psychosomatic medicine and the exploration of psychophysical analogies the sense and meaning of various skin reactions are more carefully noted.

Yet, before we describe the pathology of camouflage and disguise in more detail, we have to answer the semantic question as to whether we are allowed to use the term 'communication' in referring to these manifestations. Communication is an intentional act – some goal has to be reached, some message has to be transmitted from one creature to another. Or, to say it in different words, communication is the bridging of interindividual space. In the entire animal kingdom many nearly unexplored forms of signs and transmission signals are used in the service of mood-conveyance. From the dancing movements of the bee, the mystery of the homing instinct in birds, and the use of special colors, smells, or excrements in various higher mammals, we learn that gradually a system of overt attitudes, sound alarms, and warnings develops that may very well approach the realm of preverbal human communication. The concepts of camouflage and mock-behavior are of great importance for the study of archaic communication. Even though men do not exactly change the coloring of their skins, or roar in a frightening way as lions do, they exhibit comparable forms of behavior in their verbal communication. Instead of biological masks, they use word masks and hide their thoughts and feelings behind fine-sounding clichés. The strategy of verbal confusion is often used as a disguise for ignorance. The inflection or overemphasis of our words and the repeated roaring of the same clichés have acquired an identical defensive meaning as the threatening noises in the animal kingdom. Military experience tells us that soldiers shot their rifles more frequently as a noisy defense against their own fear than as a means of hitting a target. Many of our so-called nervous habits are part of various gestural expressions, mostly symbolic in content, but often containing primitive defensive signals.[17] Linguists increasingly tend to explain parts of man's verbal development and habits as a transformation of earlier gestural communication. Even the most phlegmatic philosopher or psychologist increases his gestural movements when he wants to emphasize his words. When attacking his audience, he stands aggressively upright, but he ducks and shrugs his shoulders when he must concede a point in a discussion. Similarly, some of our neurotic patients speak a gesture language which can be analyzed as easily as their verbal associations. One of my woman patients always walked in a bent-over fashion as if ducking something; she did this unconsciously to hide her breasts and her femininity.

A special problem of archaic communication presents itself when we consider the nearly unexplored channels of extrasensory transfer of stimuli which are being investigated by the students of parapsychology.[15] The facts show that there is a continual, non-symbolic, direct transfer of feelings among men and throughout the entire animal world.

THE PATHOLOGY OF THE SIGNALING SKIN

Do rudimentary forms of communication play a role in human pathology? The problem is important because in several forms of mental and bodily regression – when in danger a primitivization of human reactions takes place – a host of such archaic reactions or presymbolic and preverbal communications may make their appearance.

For the psychiatrist this subject is of special importance because the human body continually expresses, in a somatic way, inner emotional activity. This may take place directly through archaic alarm signals – as, for instance, yawning, infantile grasping, stretching, brow wrinkling and smiling – or in a more complicated, symbolic way as the result of training and conditioning,[12] as we see in tics, blisters, warts, furuncles, and so forth. Of importance is the fact that a continual appeal for help may be expressed through body symptoms. Our physical survival is in part determined by our communicative exchange with our fellow men, or by the opposite compulsion to deny or camouflage these signs and signals. The appeal for pity and more intensive coddling, for instance, may be expressed by the baby in numerous colds. When, however, his quest is not well received by the parents, he has to develop some other form of expression and communication of his needs or eventually fall back on repression and frustration. I would like to draw specific attention to various types of skin activity which may sometimes be called rudimentary forms of human mimicry. These manifestations are observed during psychotherapy with neurotics and psychotics. Rudimentary, biological functions may also play a role in many unexplained dermatological manifestations such as neurodermatitis, rosacea, melanosis.

One of the better-known examples of such a twofold archaic warning signal is itching. It warns the individual, but the resulting scratching gives the observer the creeps. Although the physiologist explains this manifestation as being caused by a proteolytic enzyme in the skin – without explaining its contagious action – our common experience is that the primary sensory signal may reveal either a beginning disease such as diabetes or some inner emotional action about to begin. We are itching to do something. In several of my patients their so-called pruritus broke out when they tried to repress acute anger. The tingling sensation of itching excites us. We may even be 'tickled to death.' Psychologically, itching is related to the infant's need for skin satisfaction, or the aggressive need to scratch somebody the infant identifies with. Therefore, itching and scratching can become completely sexualized, often leading to a dermal orgasm which disappears when a normal outlet for anger or sex is found. In some cases of schizophrenia we can observe phases of itching and incessant, hostile scratching, especially along the erotogenic zones, often leading to bruising and inflammation of the itching skin. Yet neurotics can also get a lot of masochistic pleasure out of continuous itching and scratching. Their communication is always an ambivalent one. Besides the quest for increased affection, there exists a camouflage of sadistic fantasies. One of my patients experienced a renewal of eczema of the hands only when childhood fantasies of choking his brother returned.

In the already mentioned case of archaic camouflage, the fear-melanosis, we nowadays understand better the chemical relation between the archaic protective coloration of the skin and the overactivity of the adrenal corticoid and sympathetic defense systems. We see, for instance, the same more diffuse pigmentation in Addison's disease. Further study of these archaic reactions may supply a better understanding of the link between deepseated panic, hormonal mobilization, and the exacerbation of some malignant tumors such as melanoma. Clinically, this link seems to be established.[14] The nevus appears to be sensitive to increased emotional skin activity and the hormone involved, MSH (melanocytestimulating hormone) is determined as intermedium, part of the huge ACTH complex.* Intermedin darkens the skin in pregnancy, affects night vision, causes daily variations of skin pigmentation with stress, and changes the pigmentation of the eye. This separate hormone can darken the skin of frogs, fish, and other animals just as ACTH can.

We often find the contrasting function of dermal alert and disguise in various pathological skin signals. The skin weeps in transudation or eczema and flushes in rosacea. In hypnosis and autohypnosis it can show the strangest symptoms, such as artificial blisters, or the bloody stigmata of the saints (i.e., sweating blood).

But utter infantile dependency, coupled with a quest for loving skin care, can also be expressed through eczema. Many dermatoses unconsciously express the need for continual skin contact and skin protection, such as the infant experienced in the womb, or the need for affection and attention. One finds such dermatoses frequently occurring in rejected (institutionalized) children. [24] One of my patients, an alcohol addict, developed eczema only when he was 'dried up.' Under the influence of his drinks (and drugs) he was easily able to regress emotionally to the nirvanic psychic state of the womb. In periods of abstention, however, he acted out his dependency needs with 'weeping' skin symptoms and other hypochondriac complaints which he often overtly expressed in his dreams. His oral craving for food and narcotics

* Dr. Choh Haoh Li and associates in the *Journal of the American Chemical Society*, Sept. 4, 1956.

was an expression of his passive wish to be loved, of a receptive longing to be taken care of forever. In his abstention periods his exposed and wounded skin took over the role of the helpless, vulnerable infant.

The skin is also the organ of embrace and contact and many dermatoses may express an ambivalent feeling toward such skin intimacy.

Often skin symptoms and their consequent need for scratching are used as a substitute for masturbation, replacing the quest for a deeper need of love and care. Only in the last decade have we learned to realize how dependent the infant is on caressing and skin stimulation.[1]

Many dermatological patients pamper their skin so 'overlovingly' that the dermatologist has only to take away their arsenal of ointments to attain a final cure. The underlying unconscious fantasy – as some of my patients revealed in their dreams – was that of shedding their skin, of tearing away this organ that prevented the symbiotic fusion with the mother. Indeed, there exists an infantile wish to fuse with the mother, combined with the opposing fear of being swallowed up. Therefore, some dermatoses were an expression of defense *against* this wish for incestuous skin contact, as I have observed in some latent homosexuals. In several patients with an emotional skin rash I found the Bible story of Jonah and the whale repeatedly appearing in their dream life as a panicky, ambivalent fantasy of skin delight and skin destruction while living in a fantasy womb.

Another form of skin communication is found in the appearance of acne. In patients in analysis, or in those receiving psychotherapy, it is almost invariably an expression of a search for skin gratification with consequent greater sexual fulfillment, the paradoxical wish to be kissed and touched *in spite of* the repelling inflammation. In adolescence, with its turmoil of feelings about sex problems, the breaking out of an eruption of acne is experienced as shame, but at the same time as a less conscious defense against being looked at as a sexual partner. In three cases of acne necrotica in adolescence which I treated, there was overt anxiety about exposed inner sexual feelings. Only psychotherapy was able to break the vicious relationship between fear of acne and its increasing activity. When, however, a loveless, withdrawn patient in psychotherapy begins to get acne, it often expresses the return of long-repressed feelings.

In schizophrenic symptomatology archaic skin behavior and archaic skin communication may play a paradoxical role. A schizophrenic patient of mine was always picking her skin. This caused her secondary trouble through inflammation. The picking was explained by her as removing the place of possible contact with other people and the outer world. Sometimes we observe an orgy of picking in patients who try to act out all kinds of repressed anal symptoms. The blackhead (comedo) plays a role in many a compulsion neurosis. By calling attention to their skin reaction the patients are often able to establish better contact with the therapist. In the case of one of my patients there was verbal contact only as long as the skin disease, an eczema, lasted. It was as if the therapist were allowed to communicate only through the open pores of the skin. As soon as the skin was healed, the psyche was closed off.

I have asked special attention for skin pathology because clinically and therapeutically we experience more and more that in cases of such dermatoses, the artificial dependency brought about by hypnotic regression and hypnocatharsis clarifies and substitutes for the deeply rooted infantile needs of the patient. Gordon published a case of a somatically incurable dermatitis herpetiformis, cleared up rather rapidly by deep hypnosis.[6]

THE MENTAL CONTAGIOUSNESS OF ARCHAIC BEHAVIOR

It is important to be aware of the contagiousness and the empathy-provoking action of archaic signs. We ourselves may feel an itching sensation when the above mentioned symptoms are brought up in conversation by patients or others. Many people cannot see eczema without becoming itchy themselves. The more a human expression approaches an undifferentiated archaic form, the more unobtrusive is the communicative meaning it conveys. Laughter, crying, yawning, stretching, shivering, may directly evoke in us similar archaic responses.[12] There is something in the observation of such archaic behavior, of such a rudimentary sign system, that pushes us unwittingly back into our own reminiscences, as do rhythm, sounds, smells, the relaxed fetal position, dancing, and artistic creation. The common regressive fantasy provokes a deep resonance and may lead to a direct identification with the fellow being. This factor of unconscious identification through archaic signs and gestures is being exploited in political strategy, where use is made of its contagious action. Uniforms, rhythmic marching, specific gestures (Nazi salute) turned the German youth more easily into mechanically fighting automatons.

Just as all of us are contagiously affected by yawning – which in itself may be explained as a rudiment of fetal drinking and a sign of oral yearning – so do we find other regressive symptoms easily leading to mental contagion and primitive identification. Among the Malayans, for instance, an infectious imitation compulsion is observed as a response to fear and panic, called *Lattah*. In their despair and anxiety and their need to be inconspicuous, these people are affected by every communicative sign of the first person they meet. They identify completely with him. They follow, imitate him passively; all his movements are repeated. And when another man crosses his path, the Lattah patient starts to follow and imitate that person. As a reaction to danger and fear these people lose the distinction between the outside and the inner world. They feel, as they reveal after their panic has subsided, completely equalized and identified with the other person and his environment. Other people may start following their imitation compulsion so that gradually a whole group moves in rhythmic automatic imitation until somebody breaks the spell.

In people who had survived a catastrophe such as bombing or confinement in a concentration camp we could observe comparable archaic signals of automatic, imitative behavior as a form of camouflage against outside danger. The unconscious urge to imitate is repeatedly found in groups; we may explain it as a protective magic need to be inconspicuous.

The phenomenon of 'freezing,' also called catalepsy, can be compared with other motoric manifestations of mimicry and camouflage in the animal kingdom. Especially in birds we find such cataleptic blending with the surroundings. The bittern in his polelike, immobile posture resembles the reeds in which he stands. This stillness as a defense, as we also observe in cataleptic caterpillars and hypnotized pigeons, is equally evident in endangered and frightened human beings. In people, however, this paralysis with resulting immobilization is often experienced as an expression of opposite inner drives. The man who wants to attack and flee at the same time remains caught between his contrasting tendencies. Nothing is as contagious as this fear catalepsy. During the Second World War, I repeatedly saw how people in so-called shock (catalepsy-death attitude) aroused greater fear in those around them than the actual bombing and destruction. After plane and train accidents it is difficult to overcome the sudden immobilization reactions of some passengers and to curtail their influence on other passengers who may be more ready for active escape.

NEW HORIZONS IN THE THEORY OF COMMUNICATION

Are we allowed to build new assumptions on these clinical examples and analogies? This is only then permitted when we can gather additional facts from more elaborate research.

I present these experiences not as final data but merely to open a chapter of clinical observation in which we need a more extensive study of phylogenesis and ontogenesis of what we may call the archaic roots of language and communication. Camouflage, the need to be anonymous and inconspicuous, the identification with the environment, play a definite role in the system of human communication. Our very posture, our thinness or obesity, can be used as tokens of camouflage.

What horizons may be opened by such new questions? What do we know, for instance, about the communicative function of breathing? Yet it is through breathing that people sustain their most archaic contact with one another. Inspiration is, as it were, inhaling 'the world' that the other fellow exhales. An asthma patient spoke about the air as the common placenta we all live from. Her unconscious fantasy about breathing made it a very threatening act.

Feelings of suffocation arouse the most contagious acts of breathing. So does clearing one's throat as an expression of hostility. Listen during an intermission at a concert when people unwittingly try to communicate their spellbound tensions or their aggressive feelings by means of contagious coughing sounds! All this may be of importance for the exploration of asthma and its equivalents, especially in those cases where psychologically deep forms of dependency are expressed.

The psychology of breathing, panting, and sighing is a neglected chapter in our books on communicative and contagious behavior.

As every clinician knows, our body can express as well as deny signs of disease. This ambivalence in clinical symptomatology is nearly unexplored. Yet, in regression and disease man's rudimentary alarm system – with its revealing and camouflaging tendency – becomes activated and may even provoke behavioral contagion through mutual identification. Mental contagion and psychological mass infection are based for the most part on these forms of unobtrusive communication.

In psychosomatic medicine we actually use the concept of organ language, by which is meant the symbolic function of organs and the appearance of disease as expression of different cultural conditioning. The new field of comparative geopathology will in the end finally explain why different diseases occur among different social and geographical groups. I am convinced, however, that the phylogenetically older systems of warning, camouflage, and communication play an important role in the final outcome of such organ language.

SUMMARY

A comparison is made between passive camouflage and its unobtrusive contagious action upon animals and men.
Archaic communication may be defined as the rudimentary remnants of animal signals originally used as warning signs for fellow creatures to flee or to hide, as means of mood conveyance or to transmit a state of alarm. Communication as a behavioral reply to an external event is the forerunner of our speech and verbal communication. This phylogenetic, older system of warning and communication still plays an important role in the symbolic function of organs and the way disease is used as a disguise or an appeal for help and pity. In regression and disease man's rudimentary alarm system becomes activated. Examples of such signs are given, such as fear melanosis, fainting, goose flesh, and several types of dermatoses. The comparative study of these rudimentary sign systems may open a new approach to the understanding of symptoms.

REFERENCES

1. ASHLEY MONTAGU, M.F., The sensory influence of the skin. *Texas Rep. Biol. & Med.* 11, 1953.
2. BRUNNER, H., Sudden whitening of hair doubted. *Science Digest, March,* 1956.
3. CRITCHLEY, M., *The Language of Gesture.* London, Arnold, 1939.
4. DARWIN, C., *The Expression of the Emotions in, Man and Animals.* (London, 1890) New York, Philos. Libr., 1955.
5. FREUD, A., *The Ego and the Mechanisms of Defense.* New York, Internat. Univ. Press, 1946.
6. GORDON, H., *Brit. M. J.,* 1955.
7. GRINKER, R.R., *Toward a Unified Theory of Human Behavior.* New York, Basic Books, 1954.
8. KAPLAN, H., and REID, M., Universal alopecia: A psychosomatic appraisal. New York J. Med., 1952.
9. KEPECS, Y.G., *et al.,* Relationship between certain emotional states and exudation into the skin. *Psychosom. Med.* 13, 1951.
10. KROLL, M., *Die Neuropathologischen Syndrome.* Berlin, Springer, 1929.
11. LORUS, J., and MILNE, M.J., How animals change color. *Scient. Am.,* 1950.
12. MEERLOO, J.A.M., Archaic behavior and the communicative act. *Psychiatric Quart.* 29, 1955.

13. MEERLOO, J.A.M., *Communication and Conversation*. New York, Internat. Univ. Press, 1952.
14. MEERLOO, J.A.M., Psychological implications of malignant growth. *Brit. J.M. Psychol.* 27, 1954.
15. MEERLOO, J.A.M., Telepathy as a form of archaic communication. *Psychiatric Quart.* 23, 1949.
16. MEERLOO, J.A.M., Eine Psychiatrische Exkursion Ueber das Medizinische Denken. *Z. Neur.* 131, 1931.
17. MEERLOO, J.A.M., Die Abwehrreaktionen des Angstgefuehls. *Z. Neur.* 133, 1931.
18. MEERLOO, J.A.M., The fate of one's face. *Psychiatric Quart.* 30, 1956.
19. MOHR, C.E., *Camouflage in Nature*. Garden City, N. Y., Doubleday, 1955.
20. MOULYN, A.C., Purposeful and Non-Purposeful Behavior. *Philosophy of Science* 18, 1951.
21. SAINSBURY, P., Gestural movement during psychiatric interview. *Psychosom. Med.* 17, 1955.
22. SCHJERNING, H., *Handbuch der Aerztlichen Erfahrungen in Weltkrieg*. Leipzig, Thieme, 1920.
23. SCHNEIRLA, T.C., 'Comparative Psychology.' *Encyclopedia Britannica*, 1948.
24. SPITZ, R.A., 'Hospitalism.' In *The Psychoanalytic Study of the Child*, 1945, Vol. I.
25. STEPHENSON, E.N., and STEWARD, C., *Animal Camouflage*. England, Penguin, A. 147, 1946.
26. TINBERGEN, N., *The Study of Instinct*. Oxford, Clarendon, 1951.
27. TINBERGEN, N., 'Psychology and Ethology as Supplementary Parts of a Science of Behavior.' In *Group Processes*. New York, Macy Foundation, 1955.
28. WEINSTEIN, E.A., and KAHN, R.L., *Denial of Illness*. Springfield, Thomas, 1955.
29. WOLFF, C., *A Psychology of Gesture*. London, Methuen, 1948.
30. ZAIDENS, S.H., The skin: Psychodynamic and psychopathologic concepts. *J. Nerv. & Ment. Dis.* 113, 1951.

3. The Network of Communication*

A PSYCHOLINGUISTIC ANALYSIS OF SPEAKING
AND LISTENING

INTRODUCTION

The fact that we have come together at this meeting in an ex-
pectant atmosphere of listening and talking, of speaking and hearing, with all the preconditioned anticipations of what will or will
not be talked about, gives a certain social structure to our meeting.
The conditioning starts the moment the printed announcement
of a lecture is read. It continues when the chairman introduces
the speaker, usually giving a subtle direction to what the program
will offer. Unobtrusively we are already caught in a network of
multifarious mutual intercommunication. The established feedback between speaker and audience helps to determine what will
be communicated. *My* freedom to speak here implies in part
your obligation to listen – unless you are disciples of the 'who
listens?' doctrine. The analysis of our communication network
is not a simple matter and grows ever more complicated. The
limitations which our education imposes on us, our theoretical
dogmas, our differences in social background, the conventional
words and ideas we are bound to, our accents, the manifold
relations we already have – all these diversities can be part of a
rich structure of intercommunication, but they can also become
a hindrance for mutual rapport.

---

* Read before the *Association for the Advancement of Psychotherapy*, November 20,
1959.

Man's psychologic problems come into being the moment he becomes typically human: when he reaches that point in his biologic development after which he can no longer compare his behavior with that of animals. Man, the repressed animal – or rather, man the neurotic animal – with his duality of biologic and psychologic existence, has gone through ages of instinctual repression. As we observe in children, speech gradually becomes a substitute for motoric expression and body behavior.

Later in life it functions as a deterrent on the acting out of instinctual urges. The word, in short, becomes more meaningful than the act. What better way is there, then, to understand human behavior and man's differentiations from animal life than through the study of man's specific human way of communication: his verbal exchange, his language?

Man's treasury of words represents a condensation of his history. *And it is only man's personal history and the history of the human race that can, in final analysis, be the study basis of man's behavior.* Yet, as Korzybski said, we don't have to explore man's *entire* history through all the ages, since we have in his verbal communications and word abstractions a time-condensed representation of his behavior, while in much of man's non-verbal contact and biologic sign behavior, time-condensed biologic adaptation reactions come to the fore.

The science of psycholinguistics is still in its infancy. Today's anthropologists are exploring it more extensively than the formal linguists. Freud himself described his great interest in this endeavor in several papers, and contributed greatly to it through his discovery of unconscious and condensed symbolic communication. As he told us, it was the linguistic facts that opened to him the secrets of the dream. The *word* not only is a clear and intelligent semantic sign but is also rooted in the primary process of unconscious imagery. Inflection, choice, and order of words are all related to variations of human behavior, variations of feelings and of thinking.

Tonight, however, I want to play with the *word* 'communication,' and analyze the complicated network of communication surrounding us. It is a double task. I have to investigate communication itself while I also have to communicate those very findings. Our meeting itself, with its subtle intercommunication, becomes, as it were, our laboratory. Every lecture is a conglomeration of verbal and non-verbal acts. This situation is parallel to what goes on in the therapeutic relationship and also in social conversation.

Many other scientific disciplines beside psychology are at present giving attention to the function of human rapport. Mathematicians, especially those around the school of cybernetics, and then of course the linguists, are just as much interested in this subject as we are.

The simplest definition of communication is the act of passing on information from one system to another. A sender or transmitter encodes a message; a receiver or listener decodes it. How it is done and how it can be imposed better is a technical question, usually referring to a clearer, shorter, and more economical transmission. The synapses in our central nervous system are, for instance, much lazier in their conduction than electronic computers. Here we run into our first dilemma. The technician tells us that a simple magnetic tape transmits faster and with more accuracy than the printed page. The tape contains not only the word symbols of the speaker but also his rhythm and the sound of speech both of which disappear in printed communication. This is true when seen purely from a technical standpoint. Psychologically, however, there can be an overdose of emotional noise and interference in sounds as well as in gestures which might distract from the clear semantic meaning of the printed word. Each system of transfer has its pro's and con's. Our professional awareness of an added unconscious distortion of the message makes our specific problem of psychologic communication different from the technical one, though both are interrelated.

Take, for instance, the key words *information* and *information theory*. Physicists relate the process of transferring information to the process of entropy, the way in physics some structural principle is transferred or transported from one entity to another at the cost of energy. Man's emotional temperature can be very hot indeed. Psychologically, however, human communication is a two-way transport, a mutual transfer. The information the speaking and listening entities select and acquire usually depends on the information they want to get rid of or to obtain. Lovers give each other plenty of information although their code is often a very silent one. An analysis of their magnetic tape of conversation will probably lack any semantic clarity.

When I first arrived in the United States, my simple questionings or my verbal love-making were invariably answered with an amiable: 'Uh-huh,' or 'Okay,' little noises with quite a variety of meanings.

What people transmit to each other as feeling or meaning, or information, or mere need for togetherness, is written in a key, the decoding of which is far beyond the receptive quality of magnetic tape. After all, our psychologic paradox of information and communication is expressed by the tremendous meaning of silence, by the impact of disguise and camouflage of our communicative habits, and by the function of our psychic defenses against giving or receiving information. Especially in psychotherapy we so often experience that communication and verbal noise only become intentional information when neurotic blocks have been overcome.

Information is impossible without the help of special social organizations that structure our communicative systems – or, to say it in psychoanalytic terms, no communication is possible without an established system of transference attitudes. To say it in other words, our network of communication is limited by our social grouping and the habits and prejudices inherent to them. Unobtrusively our social habits hamper our freedom of insight. Even gestures vary in different groups. Yet we can only then communicate when plain information has been accumulated. But for every one of us, reception as well as absorption of information can be interfered with by previously obtained information. We all have our dogmatic blocks and use different terms because we went to different schools.

I once had a patient who gave me the silent treatment for more than six months. Three times a week he came to me to see if I could stand his silence. As a child he had been drowned in words by a hypomanic mother and later he had been hurt many times more by therapists who used sophisticated words and false explanations, reminding him of the way his mother had punished him with her verbal overabundance. There are such things as verbal beatings which are as painful as physical punishment.

At this very moment I am aware of making abundant noises myself, while wondering meanwhile, 'How will my listeners accept my information?' 'What am I doing to my audience?' 'What web of intercommunication keeps us caught?' However, in our meeting ritual, we need a repeated transmission of clear or obtuse information in order to keep our scientific group together. Am I merely a link in this togetherness program?

Speaker and audience enter this meeting with their conscious and unconscious expectations their prejudices and prearranged affirmations. Even a lecture demands a certain initial transference and some submissiveness on the part of the listeners. Because we belong to the same 'society' or 'association,' a scientific jargon may have unwittingly developed between us, perfectly understood by all insiders. However, what I say here may be differently received in another group whose prejudices about subjects and speakers differ from ours. At our meetings we inadvertently and temporarily share special value systems and specific rhetoric and cognitive structures. The speaker, as it were, pushes you into it.

In order to increase the unity and receptive structure of his audience, the speaker must not consider his listeners a passive group. He must continually try to arouse response, rapport, and feedback. He can do this by letting his audience laugh, by using pauses, *even* by being repetitious. Some make use of aggressive emphasis. I remember a political speaker who always pounded his fist right *through* the desk. Boredom and ennui also can arouse a magic spell of passive acceptance in the audience, and it is good to realize that – more specifically in some religious communities and church audiences – the magic of ununderstood words and speeches gives some hearers the feeling of being nearer to God. I have the feeling that we therapists are sometimes tempted to use our sophisticated nomenclature in a similar way, for word-fetishes – especially the big, long words – have a soothing, magic action. Speakers use these words as a show of omnipotence. Listeners nod and pretend to understand although in reality they only succumb to the magic spell. Words often cannot tolerate the burden of their meaning; their usefulness decays. Take the word, 'schizophrenia.' It means very little anymore, yet it is the only word to attract psychiatric audiences.

But even in scientific communication – and especially in psychology – we have to exaggerate our points. Our ears usually don't tolerate the subtle nuances of meaning. I myself tend to vulgarize and emotionalize expression. I want to appeal without provoking too much mirth, otherwise I would destroy the subtlety of my point. Not long ago I had to take part in a panel discussion with four colleagues. Three of us had prepared our notes carefully; the fourth and last discussant had not prepared himself at all; he did not stick to the point, but launched his jokes all over the place. Yet this man had the attention of the audience. I have taken part in panel discussions where all of us hastily tried to shovel our verbal food into the mouths of the listeners who were soon all 'fed up.' You see: it was a discussion on hostility and aggression.

What is my motivation for speaking tonight? The search for prestige? Exhibitionism? Curiosity? Defense? The need to communicate? The need to convert you and to make you change your opinion? Do I really have something to say? Is there an unintentional conveyance of my own mood?

There exists a tremendous make-believe in our scientific interests. We may come here *as if* we wanted to listen, *as if* we were enjoying the meetings, *as if* we had something to say. At some meetings, facts and precision are what the audience wants to hear; an emotional and philosophical empathy with the speaker is the object of other meetings. All these motivations and more play a role in my case as I stand here tonight. Every scientific society is somehow also a garrulity center, a mutual admiration society, and has some inadvertent motivation to exclude or reject others.

About the way we meet each other compulsively at scientific gatherings it can be said that various listeners come with different motivations. The extrovert needs companions to make his system of communication more harmonious; the introvert mostly communicates with his own memories and inner gestalts. There are, also, those who come to meetings only to sleep under the guise of sophistication: the wish for a hypnotizing, soothing voice arouses reminiscences of their parents in early days. Others come to verify their preconceived theory with what the speaker has to say, or want to be gratified in some more passive, persuasive need. Yet another group wants to wait till the discussion period starts to vent professional frustration, for after all, our meeting is also a market for different opinions. And every speaker takes part unobtrusively in that subtle play of unaware tendencies. He may sway the audience or the audience may push him to say what is not true, or lead him to slander some publicly known scientific scapegoat. As a scientist I have to be careful not to make use of sudden interjections and examples induced by my temporary emotional state. Yet such outbursts usually enhance communicative rapport. I can be forced to quote the adored idols in psychology – full of awe and affirmation – I can also be directed to quote them while giving a disparaging slant to what I am saying, which, combined with appropriate grimaces, temporarily destroys their words. I can also use words such as *ego*, *cathexis*, *schizophrenia*, or *sublimation* in a magic way as if they contained every solution. He who has the magic word has magic power: he is the master of the Name!

Nobody is unconditionally open to the speaker. There is always a complicated system of feedbacks that change and distort and even annihilate the information given. The important question is: what do we in final instance get out of this meeting? What do we accumulate as new information? What is rejected or not absorbed?

One of my teachers in philosophy had the gift of taking his audience up into his height of thinking. Though we could not reproduce his words afterwards, the essence of his thinking was transferred to us.

The timing of information is also of importance. A precocious theory, however good it may be, does not find the right hearing, while a speaker can also be too late with the presentation of his point of view. Even in the central nervous system different impulses arrive at a different time and block later impulses.

An important role is played by the inadvertent credibility the audience invests in the speaker. You may call it transference. Acknowledgment often depends more on the receptivity of the public than the factual information the speaker has to offer. He can have applause and success without anybody really listening: often a speaker catches the ears but not the minds of his listeners. The story occurs to me about the wife of a famous mathematician who always went to her husband's seminars. When a colleague wanted to discuss with her some theorems, she blushingly admitted that she didn't know anything about math but only went because her husband displayed the nicest dimples in his face during such discussions.

COMMUNICATION AS A TRIAL AND ERROR TECHNIQUE

Indeed, it is very difficult to get our private points across. That is why it is generally better to use a certain naiveté of expression. Or we can quote at length. Quotation-mania is a peculiar defense mechanism in our scientific battle for security: 'He said it before I said it before, so it still holds true when I say it again!' The need for reference expresses in general a weakness in direct expression. I have to invoke the idols of the profession to help me to transmit my point! Are we not aware anymore that every verbal act is a plagiarism?

There is even something in the rigidity of repetitiousness that may catch the audience and coerce it into believing. An untruth repeated ten times may become an accepted truth. Theory is often the eternalization of our lack of insight. Even when the audience consciously defies the speaker because of a badly presented paper, unwittingly they may take something over from him. Many suggestions slip through the barrier of our critical defenses even when we consciously deny or even detest the speaker's words. Subliminal mental coercion is an old subject in human rapport. Many propagandists make use of this easy puncturing of man's critical defenses.

All this may happen because we listen not only with our conscious ears. We listen with our dreams and our anxieties. We not only listen with our cerebral cortex but also with our archaic subcortical centers, with our hatreds and our loves, with our delusions and our prejudices. We translate what we hear by the myth we live in. Even the dreams of our patients we translate with the subjectivity of the systems of thinking we live in. When I read about dream analysis from students of different schools, I hear different stories. We listen also with the collective structure imposed on us in every meeting of human minds. In an orthodox psychoanalytic meeting I listen differently than in a meeting for eclectic psychotherapy. There may be a stranger in our midst – of equal intelligence and seemingly speaking the same language – to whom all *we* talk about may seem like utter mumbo jumbo. In some scientific meetings I felt myself completely in the outfield, with that Kafka feeling of being in a castle without any known dimension for orientation. Every so-called objective description implies an inference and assumes a personal point of view. The pomp of our scientific words unobtrusively exerts a hypnotic action even in our own thinking. Thus we can be victimized by our temporary findings combined with our limited outlook.

There exist forms of communication which are specifically suspect. They are clothed in repetitious words and automatic clichés in which the original meaning is either lost or successfully hidden. Our science of psychology is full of these. Words like libido, psyche, allergy, third ear, integration, existence, defense are already so much used that they cover up the problems rather than clarify them. Our concepts are in a continual flux. We have to be very much aware of this fossilization of our verbal intercourse in which the need to explain everything preposterously pokes fun at us. Language and speech often serve as compensation for loss of deeper communication.

Communication is an act that involves working with several means. Every word is a trial-call. It is a play with probabilities in which we use sound and noise, rhythm and silence, semantic clarity and verbal fog. We aim multiple words at the target, hoping that somehow in the end we will have hit the bull's-eye and will have conveyed our information. Communication of any sort can almost be compared with trying to knock down a row of pins in a bowling game. The more balls we throw, the greater is the probability that we will hit all the pins. The more approaches we make to any problem the greater the chance of finding and grasping its essential core. Only the creative artists among us have that special ability of making a direct hit with a mere mouthful of words.

Our critics have found an adequate answer to this enigma of communication. They have discovered that making a caricature out of a communication helps to clarify the expression. We need our discussants and the question periods afterwards, for they provide the humoristic element that enlivens the communicative play. Far from disrupting the meeting – as I have often heard it said – they accentuate the paradoxical role of communication. Often it is not the debater but the silent listener who gets greater clarity out of this game, for remember that many people acquire understanding only after either verbalization of their own ideas, or after having heard a discussant verbalize their doubt for them. Without the freedom of discussion, they would suffer from verbal constipation.

Free communication must be a two-way road. Speaker and listener identify with each other. The standpoint of the one can be as convincing as the opinions of the other, while changing standpoints can be clarifying and illuminating. Of course, the one who yields his point of view can do it out of the need for passive mental surrender.

Our discussions are not so important because of the questions that are asked, but they stimulate the appropriate feedback mechanisms in every listener. Therefore, rash questions are as important in establishing such increased communicative aptness as the sophisticated demonstration of private wisdom.

It is the structure of the discussion that determines whether something of the meeting will remain in our minds provided there was contact with the audience, and quite independent of the amount of noise speaker and debaters may have made. But, because few have the courage to admit that they were wrong, discussion and conversation can easily become a strategic retreat from alleged verbal camouflage, constituting a deeper form of hiding that which we really mean.

A well-known member of the British Parliament once said that in the course of more than 1,000 parliamentary discussions his opinion had never changed. The use of the veto at the United Nations points at the same lack of convinceability. Usually discussion and conversation serve to justify one's own prejudice, in the semantic meaning of the word: pre=judice. Discussions consciously serve as a defense against being converted or convinced. But what really counts is the unconscious action discussions arouse.

Every speaker provokes a thousand associations in his audience, taking part himself in this web of intercommunication by over-emphasizing part of his subject and underscoring other parts. Somebody in the audience yawns and already the speaker may change his inflections. His gesture language is part of that play of comical contrasts. His talking may be very rigid and dictatorial – *you, my audience, have to swallow this* – while at the same time his gestures may laugh at his own earnestness. His movements, as it were, are belying his words. A lecture wherein there is no laughter and no comical exaggeration of the subject fails in its communicative impact.

What I have tried to communicate is that speech and verbal clarity are only part of the network of communication. There is much more unconscious and unaware transmission than words can express. I can show this best by introducing the concept of archaic communication and by showing you how much this form of rapport is still going on in our type of meetings. What we call archaic communication consists of the various signs, tokens, and signals we usually exchange without being aware of it. These are remnants from biologic signals of danger and distress, of the alarming and the warning call and of signs of mimicry and camouflage. They comprise all those rudimentary biologic communications in the service of appropriate adaptation. The pitiful call of distress can be heard coming from even the most secluded solitary animals. Our paleness, our coloring, our gestures and rhythms, our motoric behavior, our shouting and crying – all are still used in the service of such animal behavior. Because everybody is unwittingly dragged into such biologic empathy, the acts of laughing, yawning, shrieking, crying, itching, and scratching are very contagious expressions. They all have a deep communicative value, affecting us more than we care to admit. The animal's sound of distress provokes feelings of distress in us. Psychosomatic medicine may be formulated as the science of body signals in the service of normal as well as pathologic communication.

I once attended a meeting where the speaker suddenly started to stutter and grow pale. Everybody was aware of some tragedy occurring in him. Was he struck by some sad reminiscence? Was it a stroke? Happily enough, he took hold of himself, though still trembling. Later on I discovered that nearly everyone in the audience had been caught up in the strange moment and had produced his own associations and explanations of the incident.

The science of those directly contagious movements and rhythms – as a result of an unobtrusive common regression – in which vibration, smell, sound, and noise play such a tremendous role has been studied more objectively and clinically only within the last few years. But Hitler already knew how to hypnotize his audience into servile submission by many rhythmic clichés: 'Sieg Heil, Sieg Heil,' by mass-gestures, boring redundancy of words and the 'glue' of common agitation.

Psychoanalysis and all psychotherapeutic experiences familiarize the therapist with what we may call non-verbal and even unconscious communication. Although there was a time when we hesitantly put these concepts under the headings of primitive participation and regression, we now realize more than before that we are all living together in a tremendous web of intercommunication, of which we usually catch only the *crudest* clues the verbal ones.

If a hidden camera were to make a movie of this meeting and the picture were projected on the screen at fast-moving speed, we would detect various rhythmic interactions between speaker and audience, depending on the changes of emotional impact. Elsewhere I have called this the dance of conversation, because the rhytmic moving to and fro occurs in every conversation. Only a few sensitive people are able to pick up this silent rhythmic exchange. Our great creative artists have known how to express directly in form and line what could only later be conceptionalized in words.

With these examples the field of archaic communication is not yet exhausted. There are many more sensory and extrasensory stimuli that reach us without our being consciously aware of it. There are the color impressions, the speaker's tie, his clothes, the dance of that part of him that is visible behind the desk – often only the top of his skull. They are all part of the conscious and subliminal intrusion of the stimuli that reaches the audience. I want also to draw your attention to the so-called telepathic or psi-phenomena and the rules and laws of their transmission.

Such a vast statement about continual communicative intrusion is not easily accepted. The fact that our mind is continually sifting and selecting the abundance of information that comes in – even in sleep – affects our individual pride. We hate the thought that imprints are made on our minds without our consent. Yet, we have become vaguely aware of the fact that our brains send out electric waves and that somehow people are linked together not only in a huge electromagnetic continuum but also in a vast communicative continuum.

COMMUNICATION AS DISGUISE

A patient comes in talking about the awful weather in a flood of self-pitying terms. Indeed it is snowy and windy outside, but the tone of her voice indicates that she uses the weather device to hide inner turmoil that cannot yet be freely expressed. Another patient suddenly begins to talk about a newly discovered art object in my room that had been there all during the many months of her treatment. Her new discovery heralds another case of inner turmoil that cannot yet be brought to the fore out of inner darkness. A third one withholds any form of verbal conversation: she throws herself onto a chair and sits there passively, yet with a defiant air. But her tense expectation betrays the fact that an inner conversation is going on. Her facial gestures reveal her wish to express something, but somehow the words are withheld.

In every conversation we find these patterns of displacement and camouflage of what is really going on inside the mind. An inquiry into the function of such mutual exchange in various setups is needed, especially since our technical culture is invading the patterns of free mutual exchange called conversation. I have, for instance, witnessed families where as a result of radio and television the ancient art of verbal communion and conversation has completely disappeared. The various members of the family customarily retreat to different rooms to be entertained by their respective television screens. Even meals are taken separately and friends no longer are invited for cozy talk and conversation, but only to share the programs.

Many psychologic needs are satisfied in the human contact of conversation. The contact can be amusement, the wish to impress and to boast or to be brilliant, the need to exert verbal power, or the wish to be stimulated by others. Conversation is a social lubricant, a mutual exchange of tolerance and an equal sharing of honor and attention. It promotes the sense of direct understanding or provides the joy of an insignificant interchange of elated verbosity which provides the pleasure of relishing nonsense. Expressing oneself in conversation is like feeding each other words and gestures in order to relax, though hidden moods are exchanged too.

Conversation implies a mutual discharge of tensions, a mutual cathartic function through the promiscuity of words. Everybody receives a share perhaps of aggressive jokes or of soothing words. Talking and communicating have become a mutual libidinal penetration without anxiety-provoking taboos. They provide, so to say, a spontaneous group therapy.

But many interfere with those cathartic rules. There are those who like to talk only for the pleasure of hearing their own voices while continually checking other people to observe what response they provoke. Such domineering neurotics may be constantly rejected precisely because of this wrongly chosen verbal strategy. Then there are those who only listen out of a masochistic compliance. They let the words penetrate without converting them into thoughts and counter-words while inwardly they mope because they think they have no opportunity to speak. Then there are those eternal Don Juans, permanently in search of substitute mothers. They use words only as seductive tentacles. Confidential talk is often their first sexual approach: 'Please, let me show you my unconscious in exchange for yours!' And that is the beginning of their verbal promiscuity always ending in seduction.

I have known circles of neurotics where pseudo-psychiatric knowledge was bandied about and mutual psychoanalysis was misused as an introduction to verbal promiscuity, the erotic confession and sexual conversation gradually leading to physical seduction.

During the investigation of brainwashing it was of great importance to understand that the hidden erotic relation between interviewer and interviewee led to the prisoner's compliance without his being consciously aware of it. This interaction is part of our daily conversation pattern of which the therapist must be constantly aware, for it may tempt him to comply too much with the patient's wishes.

One finds various conversational types. The hyperlogicians and the continual propagandists, the joker who secretly wants to eat you, the critics, and those in never-ending search for sympathy. There are the gossipers, the hypochondriacs, the sobbers, the gigglers and the know-alls. And all these types acquire a special meaning in the therapeutic setting for they use the conversational circle to cry or they cry by proxy by making others weep.

The greatest difficulty confronts those who never manage to escape from their own logic-systems. They fight the world in order to safeguard themselves and their inner confusion. I once treated a hypochondriac professional philosopher, sent to me by his internist. He had an answer to every question. He knew a logic-system fitting every situation. But no one was ever allowed to probe his infantile yearning and self-pity. At this point he immediately escaped into angry sophisticated dialectics, a beautified logic mumbo jumbo. I could never reach the little boy in him.

Scientific circles are not always free from this escape into terminological oversophistication which is simply a device for hiding the fear of not knowing.

RESUMÉ

Let us try to pull some conclusions together.

For the process of communication and mutual information a social structuration is needed with preconceived sets of readiness to perceive what is transmitted. Also in scientific circles various groups develop different communication networks in which preconceived ideas and different receivers and senders confuse the intercommunication from one group to the other. This structural variation of prejudiced hearing and privileged nomenclature is especially highly developed among psychologists and psychiatrists. We are continually subjected to communicative stress from outside with its inherent manipulations of individual and mass opinions.

The information we want to give usually fits better and has a more enriching appeal when good rapport and initial transference exist. A libidinal factor plays an important role here. The timing of the message, the structure of the receiving individual or group, and the way the speaker manages to structure his own messages into a gestalt, a myth, a style, a theory, change the impact. Facts alone will not do. The speaker is even allowed to contradict himself because nobody is without ambivalence.

An analysis of archaic communication shows how unwittingly and unconsciously the network of rudimentary biologic signals modifies the impact of speech. All people, even the most isolated individuals, are reached and often coerced by subtle, conscious signs and subliminal stimuli. Emotional growth forces them to select those stimuli and to build up barriers of defenses.

In the total process of communication everybody makes use of various means of contact. These clusters of trial calls increase the probability that the essential core of the information will in final instance be transferred to the receivers of the message. In the total network of communications we can detect four groups of relations:

1. Man's relation to his own memories, which tends to distort his communicative system;
2. man's relation to his biologic adaptive systems, continually influencing his signaling to the outer world;
3. man's relation to the objective world, to time and space, and
4. finally, man's large set of subtle interrelationships, starting with his parents and gradually expanding to mankind.

Every understanding is an approximation through various means of communication. The network of communication usually hides the final mystery of the essence of things, because we learn to be selective with our attentions. Some day we hope to find the right names for the right things.

4. Rhythm in Babies and Adults

ITS IMPLICATIONS FOR MENTAL CONTAGION

ROCK-A-BYE BABY

The fact that the newspapers are lauding the discovery of the Sonitone-Securitone – the electronic box designed to soothe anxious tensions in young babies by imitating the sound of the maternal heartbeat – provides a motivation for reviewing what is known about man's rhythmic functions. Psychologist Lee Salk's application of maternal cardiac rhythm is rather simple. Observing that both monkeys and human babies behave more quietly when resting near the maternal heart, he postulated that an artificial reproduction of the same rhythm would have a soothing influence on the increased adjustment of neuroregulatory patterns that, after birth, were suddenly exposed to the irregular rhythms of reality. Nobody has as yet mentioned the danger inherent in an automatic mechanical device which replaces the valuable personal interaction between mother and child.*

Those who are familiar with the training of pets know that a yelping, anxious baby dog can be soothed by a ticking clock enveloped by a blanket. Rhythm, in the first place, gives a feeling of familiarity. But if the little dog depends on the automatic device only, he becomes a neurotic dog.

It must be said that many mothers intuitively apply their notion concerning the baby's need for rhythmic soothing by rocking

---

* A more thorough study of this mother-child interaction was made in an earlier article.[13]

the cradle. Hypnosis, too, starts with a rhythmic soothing of the subject. 'Rock-a-Bye Baby' and other rhythmic lullabies are as old as mankind. Observation of intrauterine behavior shows that the baby rhythmically floats † up and down in the amniotic fluid and also reacts to sound impressions from outside[5,14]; he is subjected to two kinds of rhythmic sound patterns, the maternal heartbeat and the embryonal one, with a rhythm of one to two. We may accept the fact that the intrauterine rhythmic experience is the conditioner and precursor of the rhythm acted upon later in infancy. Before birth the baby lives as it were in a syncopated sound-world, and it is easy to imagine that a reconstitution of these soundpatterns provokes mnemonic reminiscences of the past intrauterine equanimity – the lost paradise. From patients in psychotherapy we have learned that the ecstasy of jazz and rock-and-roll provokes various reminiscent moods of a lost happiness that can never be found again.

SPONTANEOUS RHYTHMIC BEHAVIOR

From the eighth intrauterine week the embryonic organism lives in a total rhythmic behavior. Rhythmic reactive and protective movements are noted. As said before, the fetus lives in a floating rhythmic soundworld filled with auditive impressions from the maternal heart and vessels, with a mean frequency of 70, and a different rhythm of its own fetal heart, with a mean frequency of 140, superimposed upon it. The fetus is observed to react also to sounds from the outside world. This observation, combined with the knowledge that amniotic fluid is a better sound conductor than air, makes the acceptance of a prenatal syncopated rhythmic sound-world more than probable. Rhythmic rocking, dancing, and floating in the amniotic fluid belaong to the well-observed normal intrauterine movements.[14] The child in the uterus yawns (intrauterine drinking), scratches, cringes, and stretches in response to outside stimulation.

As we can observe in babies born in a world not so mechanized and civilized as ours, a rhythmic motoric interaction between

† The word rhythm is derived form rheein = to flow.

mother and child develops when the child is brought to the breast and mother's body immediately after birth. Baby's hands exercise with a rhythmic pawing of the breast (the milk reflex, so clearly visible in cats when they are stroked); baby's head makes a rhythmic movement from one nipple to the other; both mother and child move to and fro in rhythmic movement. This 'milk dance' reminds one of the rhythm of coitus, as if the acts of continuity of life are governed by the same rhythmic interaction. Many mothers who breastfeed their children – especially those among primitive people – unwittingly use the same rhythmic movements every time they give the breast. Even the sucking on the part of the baby occurs rhythmically, as does the later thumb sucking. Usually these rhythmic interactions disappear when the period of breast feeding is delayed from 4 to 6 hours after birth. This suppression of rhythmic interaction is probably phylogenetically related to an adaptive nipple-seeking behavior seen in higher animals, in which the newborn is rejected by mother and flock when it can not reach the nipple within a specific time span.

Of importance for pathology is that these very early repressed rhythmic reflexes return in neurotic and psychotic children – in which, according to psychoanalytic investigation, oral deprivation and the lack of motoric pleasure became a too-overwhelming trauma. We repeatedly observe in psychotherapy that even in older patients, in analytic regression, or in deep hypnosis, early infantile rhythmic motoric patterns spontaneously return. Some adults complain about returning rhythmic contractions of the legs shortly before falling asleep.

The startle-reaction in infants also shows a pattern of rhythmic defense movements; such a startle can also burst out in a rhythmic jumping in frightened older people.

Spontaneous rocking, bouncing, headbanging, or jumping is often seen in well-cared-for infants (Mittelman's autoerotic movement[15]), usually in the first year of life; these movements can persist and be used as a masochistic self-hurting reaction to some conflictuous experience. Headbanging (*jactatio nocturna*), early masturbation, and rhythmic rocking may all be interpreted as manifestations of displaced appropriate innate rhythmic reflexes in the service of primary gratification. [2,9]

Here is where the rhythmic behavior of the mother-rocking the cradle; singing lullabies; carrying and coddling the child; holding it 'under her heart' (in the double meaning of the word) – serves to supply and guarantee feelings of security and protected dependency. Masserman[8] explains this dependency on rhythm as one of the magic ur-defenses of man, the miraculous transformation of chaos into pleasurable order. The outside rhythm is incorporated into a personal beat and time.

Man's cooscillation with the rhythm of the outside world brings him back to nirvana – the never-never-land. The rhythm of the waves of the sea has a sleep-arousing action; we surrender to the magic roaring of the sea. If people cannot live and move in unison, they get sick and seasick; the whole world is experienced as one huge piece of danger.

BIOLOGICAL RHYTHMS

But life is a conglomeration of many more rhythms, known and unknown. There have appeared various articles recently about man's built-in biological clock. Among animals we know several instances of accurate instinctual measuring of the cosmic time, without benefit of outer clocks. The lower the animal organism, the greater the parallelism of the world rhythm with its own. Fish in an aquarium rise to the surface to await their food at exactly fixed times. Certain worms of the seashore dig themselves into the sand shortly before the beginning of the flood tide. Many butterflies change their coloring with day and night. Not only the rhythm of the sun but that of the moon awakens analogous phenomena in many animals. There are worms that come out of the sand at full moon. The ancient Greek physicians were much more interested than we in the manifold rhythmic symptoms of man: 'The body consumes time by its functions.' (Hippocrates.)

Darwin thought that man coming forth from the sea must still have a tidal rhythm in him, and we must accept some interrelation between the lunar phase and the menstrual hormonal process even though the direct links are unknown. The term lunacy for mental disturbance belongs to the realm of explorable concepts of continuous geophysical action on man.[6]

Man is usually not directly aware of following cosmic rhythms. Periodic events in man come gradually under control of the autonomic nervous system, yet, the moment we start to measure body functions, e.g., man's temperature, we become aware of this cosmic rhythm. We know of the existence of hormonal rhythms, to which the menstrual cycle belongs. We are familar with a variation in moods related to the seasons and of the periodic seasonal appearance of stomach ulcer.[3] Among pathologists there is a growing tendency to relate certain periodic diseases to unknown rhythms of life (cyclic neutropenia, periodic arthralgia, periodic paralysis).[17] With the electrocardiogram, the electroencephalogram, and the electrodermatogram, normal and pathological rhythms can be discovered. Breathing has its various rhythm, the guts have, the heart has, the muscles have, the molecules have, and even the intra-atomic particles.

Bodily functions and temperature are closely coordinated with the rhythm of night and day. In some people a sudden geographical shift, e.g., after an airplane trip, brings a temporary disruption of the regular rhythm, causing tiredness and autonomic disturbances.

The rhythm of maternal schedules begins to intrude into the biological rhythms at birth. The first clock the infant hears is mother's heartbeat when lying at mother's left breast. Waiting for feeding in a hungry expectancy creates the first mnemonic impression of empty time, which plays such an important role in dreams of frustrated people. Sometimes the intrusions by artificial schedules may lead to an educational eurhythmia or a clash, a dysrhythmia. The child puts his own rhythm against someone else's rhythm. The manic-depressive vacillation of moods is often explained as such an early acquired dysrhythmia. Psychosomatic diseases often start as defense against the intrusion by outside schedules. In attempting to control the unpleasant routine, the counterroutine begins to control the protester.

Neuropathologically, we know that there is also a relation between rhythm and the archaic sense of vibration.

RHYTHM AND THE SENSE OF TIME

Of importance to our subject is the notion that all these various rhythms somehow teach man to orient himself in time.[16] Man perceives time not only because of a built-in biological clock but also because of a confrontation of inner with outer rhythms. Klages[7] explains it as the human transformation of a biological rhythm into a personal beat, an individual tune. The neutral metric rhythm becomes a musical rhythm, something personal. The automatic noises of a train acquire a personal interpolation and change into a song or a sentence.

Man's awareness of world time and his subjective judgment of time span are both related to this interaction of internal rhythm with outer rhythmic events. Hormones (thyroid), for instance, are able to change man's judgment of time span. Scientists have recently become more interested in man's inner time sense because of the possibility of space travel and its eventual danger to time experience and body rhythm.

Even in memorizing unrelated events people make a personal rhythmic event out of it. Telephone numbers are more often sung than spoken. By remembering a melody, we also remember the words. When one listens to a conversation in a language one does not understand, one becomes much more aware of the rhythmic interaction of people who exchange feelings and thoughts.

The more differentiated forms of time sense – the awareness of historicity and of duration and continuity – are related to higher cerebral development. There exists a specific pathology of such time sense in schizophrenia and cerebral diseases.[1,10]

Man's time sense is related to the impact of various rhythms from the outside; indeed, man is dependent on rhythmic interaction with the outside world. When his sensory antennae are not allowed to signal this interaction – as in the experiments with sensory deprivation – man loses all sense of time and breaks down very easily.

Though there are various rhythms active in man, many of which are gradually being discovered by physiological measurement, there is a limit to man's perception of intervals. Certain animals (e.g., gnats) are able to distinguish much smaller intervals, a 10,000th or a 15,000th of a second.

What man usually experiences as a continual occurrence – as, for instance, on the movie screen – is actually a swift succession of apparitions, of waves of tremors, of minuteous movements unknown to man's direct perception. Man is only one moment in the trillions of movements and waves.

'But I fancy that whatever might psychologically happen, between the first smile of rosy flesh and the last dull grin of bone, would remain for Him as undistinguishable as the gnat's ten or fifteen thousand wingbeats per second remain for us. I doubt whether the god of a system, or even of a single world, could sympathize with our emotions any more than we ourselves can sympathize with the life that thrills in a droplet of putrid water...' (Lafcadio Hearn, 4.)

RHYTHM, INDUCTION, AND MENTAL CONTAGION

Although we are not able at this moment to give an exact analysis of the complex symphony of rhythms living in our organism, the subject has become more and more important since we have become aware that rhythm in one person can be transferred directly to the other. This interplay and interaction can be especially observed in children; the dance of one provokess a dance in the playmate. All people experience this enforced reverberation and cooscillation in the group; few can resist the seductive action of a march during a parade. Most of the primitive rituals and revivals that make a solid deindividualized mass of the group do this by rhythmic chanting and rhythmic movements. The rhythmic taking over of sound and movement in dance and chant is already token contact. We less primitive members of the technical age are more unwittingly submitted to those contact-providing contaminating rhythms. Professional engineers of public opinion use jingles and rhythmic slogans to let their suggestions penetrate more easily into man's resistant minds. Television and movies use a variety of rhythms and tunes to involve us with the play on the screen. Political propaganda uses rhythmic slogans: 'Sieg Heil, Sieg Heil,' in Nazi Germany, or 'Duce, Duce, Duce,' in fascist Italy, to lull the masses into receptive submissive identification with the leader. Special beats and tunes catch us, we have to repeat them, we modulate them repeatedly in our minds. Our need to cheer and sing is partly a conquest of mechanical rhythms in us, partly the need to cooscillate with others and to feel at home in a group. Our word *emotion* originally meant 'being moved in a cooscillation with another being.'

We can see how deeply penetrating this rhythmic interaction is by making movies unobtrusively of various families. When the films are shown on the screen at faster than normal speed, we see a continual rhythmic moving to and fro in the conversational circle. Even the layman seeing these movies understands intuitively – without ever having studied these rhythms – where there is a harmonious interrelation and where not. The group interaction in group psychotherapy is always combined with contagious rhythmic movements.

What we call mental contagion or psychic contamination can usually be traced to a common regression, to infantile archaic physiological responses.[12] Rhythm provokes rhythm; laughter provokes laughter; fright provokes fright; distress call in one induces feelings of distress in another; scratching in one provokes itching in another. We may even reduce all these phenomena to a common rule: *The more an expression evokes infantile archaic responses of the organism – the innate biological signal code – the more infectious it is.* Such archaic communication may be defined as a rudimentary remnant of biological signals, originally used as a warning to fellow creatures to flee or hide. The implication of this rule of mental contamination is that it is so much easier to spread chaos, fury, panic, and revolution than to infect people with good example and restrained self-control.

One group of youngsters dancing rock 'n' roll forces another group to regress to some form of rhythmic interaction. In dancing, one surrenders to the rhythm of the dance music, as a magic surrender to the greater rhythmic occurrences in the world.[11] A national hymn provokes in everybody the yearning feelings of belonging to the group. Something occurs in people when they observe archaic sign behavior. An inner resonance unwittingly pushes them back into their childhood reminiscences; the shared regressive fantasy leads to mutual imitation. Regression is more contagious than progression!

Future physiology and psychopathology will have to direct greater attention to the analysis of these phenomena. The compulsive patient, for instance, cannot step out of his daily rhythm without feeling anxiety. Analytically it is known that the compulsion to repeat rhythmically is used as a defense against the shock of new impressions.

In some cases, mental contamination will be merely an induction of the same rhythm. These rhythms can be measured and tested. In music the transfer of emotions is, of course, much more complicated but it follows in principle the same rules of mental induction and cooscillation. There are soothing rhythms and exciting rhythms. But, in general, rhythm means recognition of something familiar. In olden days quacks used to pull teeth under the soothing rhythm of the drum.

Again, it is important to ask ourselves which rhythm does what? The rhythm and cadence of breathing is used in oriental countries to arouse erotic feelings in the mate, and every flirtation spontaneously makes use of this intuitive knowledge.

RHYTHM AND THE
UNIVERSAL IMITATION COMPULSION

The universal communion of archaic behavior is a principal factor in the concept of mental contagion. Because of this communion people are compelled to imitate what others act out for them.

An infectious imitation compulsion called Lattah is observed among Malayans as a response to fear and panic. In their despair and anxiety, and in their need to hide and be inconspicuous, Lattah victims adopt the communicative signs of the first person they meet. They identify with him completely, and follow and imitate him passively, repeating every movement he makes. When another person approaches, the victim will follow, imitate, and mimic that person. Yet, as soon as someone moves rhythmically in march tempo, or whistles, or even dances, this person's influence prevails. In their reaction to danger and stress, Lattah victims lose the distinction between outside and inner world. They feel, as one of them revealed to me after his panic had subsided, completely merged, equalized, and identified with the other person. Other people may be attracted by this anxious imitation compulsion, and finally an entire group may be moving in rhythmic automatic imitation until someone breaks the spell. Often this passive reaction to danger can change into a more active stampede of fury and running amok.

This gestural contagion can also be observed in ecstatic religious revivals. Some sects follow a ritual of archaic movements which leads to easier communion and participation in their special beliefs – as, for instance, the sects of the Jumpers and Shakers in Pennsylavania and Ohio at the beginning of the 19th century. The rhythm of swaying movements during prayer also induces this communion of feelings. It is the contagion of movement and the common expectation of salvation that leads to the common ecstatic experience of the '*mysterium tremendum*.' In the Greek 'mysteries,' the sacred dance and holy fury and possessedness played a contagious role. Ecstatic orgy and convulsive rage swept the masses into an epidemic of mass hysteria in which they believed themselves to be experiencing the sexual union of the gods.

In people who have survived a catstrophe such as bombing or confinement in a concentration camp, I have observed comparable signs of automatic, imitative behavior. The more the victims had lost their own feeling of identity, the more they imitated the gestural signs of others. Returned to normal circumstances, they soon lost this over-all merging and identifying behavior.

There exists in everyone a need to repeat old patterns of behavior. Man imitates others but also himself. In therapy, it is sometimes a great struggle to liberate a patient from these compulsive self-imitations. Without a therapeutic regression to the origin of his old schemes, most attempts at self-correction will fail.

RHYTHM AND CATHARSIS

As we experienced in dance epidemics, many rhythms are actively sought out to ward off tension and anxiety. Music and dance were once the first forms of magic medicine. The common regression to a mass of interacted movements gives delight and catharsis and revitalizes man in suspense, but the same man can also be seduced by rhythm to give up his ego completely.

On the other hand, there are people who, on the basis of early infantile rhythmic frustration, are unable to join in the dance movements, this common joy as old as mankind. They are motorically frustrated, and do not understand gestures and pantomime. However intelligent they may be, they are excluded from a large field of human intercommunication.

Music reflects to us the symphony of rhythms that we are ourselves. Rhythm is life, the tune is the mind. In the rhythm and repetition of themes in music, emotional abreaction takes place. The handling of counterpoint by composers evokes in listeners their own contrasting feelings and this harmony of contrasts temporarily frees them from inner tension. The rhythm of music can completely revolutionize our body system. The composer may inhibit us and provoke frustration with his rhythms and then, suddenly, liberate us. But this can work 2 ways: There is panic in the flute of Pan!

RÉSUMÉ

I want to emphasize the importance of the study of cycles, periodicity, and various rhythms in man and mankind. Yet, at this moment, we do not know enough of its complications and counter indications to start a well-balanced rhythmic therapy, or even music therapy of the mind. Dance therapy in psychotics usually has a liberating action followed by greater self-acceptance. The young baby already undergoes frustrations in rhythmic expression and interaction with his environment. Sometimes interaction may mean coercion, sometimes harmony and liberation. Part of our timesense is related to this interaction of rhythms, cycles, and frequencies. Neurological and emotional frustration influences man's system of intercommunication.

What at this moment looks rather complicated and is usually handled under the heading of mental contagion and psychic infection may in its simplest roots be a result of induction and coosciliation of various rhythms, so easily transmitted from one entity to another.

REFERENCES

1. EISSLER, K. R., Time Experience and the Mechanism of Isolation, Psychoanal. Rev. 39 : 1, 1952.
2. FITZHERBERT, J., Some Further Observations on Headbanging and Allied Behavior, J. Ment. Sci. 98 : 330, 1952.
3. GEORGI, K., Psychophysische Korrelationen: Psychiatrische Probleme im Lichte der Rhythmusforschung, Schweiz Med. Wschr. 77 : 1276, 1947.
4. HEARN, L., A Japanese Miscellany, Tokyo, Tuttle Company, 1954.
5. HOOKER, D., The Prenatal Origin of Behavior, Lawrence, Kansas, University of Kansas Press. 1952.
6. INMAN, W.S., The Moon, the Seasons, and Man, Brit. J. Med. Psychol. 24 : 267, 1951.
7. KLAGES, L., Vom Wesen des Rhythmus, Kampen auf Sylt, Kampman Verlag, 1934.
8. MASSERMAN, J.H., Say Id Isn't So – with Music, in Science and Psychoanalysis, New York, Grune & Stratton, Inc., 1958.
9. MEERLOO, J.A.M., Archaic Behavior and the Communicative Act, Psychiat. Quart. 29 : 60, 1955.
10. MEERLOO, J.A.M., The Psychology of Time Sense, in The Two Faces of Man, New York, International Universities Press, Inc., 1954.
11. MEERLOO, J.A.M., The Dance – from Ritual to Rock and Roll, New York, Chilton Company, 1960.
12. MEERLOO, J.A.M., Mental Contagion, Amer. J. Psychother. 13 : 66, 1959.
13. MEERLOO, J.A.M., The Atomization of the Family, Amer. Practit. 10 : 11, 1959.

14. MINKOWSKI, M., Neurobiologischen Studien am Menschlichen Foetus, Handbuch. Biol. Arbeitsmethoden, Vol. 5, 1928.
15. MITTELMAN, B., Intrauterine and Early Infantile Motility, in The Psychoanal. Study Child 15 : 104, 1960.
16. PIAGET, J., *Le developpement de la notion du temps chez l'enfant*, Paris, Alcan, 1946.
17. REIMAN, H.A., Periodic Disease, J.A.M.A. 166 : 141, 1951.

5. Mental Contagion and The Unobtrusive Manipulation of the Mind

The mind of man is never isolated. His feeling, thinking and creating are bound to mankind by a million ties. The very word he speaks was taught to him, the theory he expounds is to a certain degree a harmless form of plagiarism. The image he creates is composed of numerous images received and perceived somewhere in his past.

The inadvertent pressure on man's senses increases day by day, not only because of the expansion of his actual environmental world, but also through the elaborate mechanized forms of communication, through press, radio, movies, television. Nobody can pretend any more to be the principal originator of *his* own thinking. Inadvertently, he is enforced to absorb a thousandfold suggestions and explanations.

Actually, there exists an elaborate system of selection among all these suggestions from outside. There is affirmation, denial, or critical repudiation. We cannot merely say that people are the sum total of all the personal contacts they make, or a cross-section of the imaginary heap of persuasions which they gather in their 'inner society.' We could, in this instance, call man the sum total of *internalized* influences from outside.

As a rule, psychoanalysis and psychotherapy make people more aware of the various persons they inwardly talk to: parents, relatives, friends, foes, teachers, idealized leaders. Most of these internal communications take place unobtrusively and unconsciously.

What individual man is able to do with the web of communication around him and within himself determines how vulnerable or how strong, he will become. The communicative system within him – as represented by his nervous and hormonal systems – may act in a disturbed way, or the web of communication from outside may be inharmonious.

In a study of mental infection we must be aware of the fact that conscious and intentional communication is often not as effective as the unconscious, so-called 'preverbal' communication. Those people who are able to give direction and emotional content to other people's silent moments have more influence than those who use sophisticated words.

People are in constant psychic exchange with one another on various levels of awareness. In every personal contact it is not only the language which transmits feelings and thoughts, but the greater part of our communication is effected through minute clues of which people usually are not aware. Public opinion engineers try to utilize those clues and may even advertise using them subliminally so as to bypass man's barriers of skepticism and criticism. Gestures, tones, sounds, silences, and irritations in response to special words often have a greater impact than words, grammar and syntax. In the past few years, psychiatry has paid more attention to the subject of non-verbal communication because it is of such vital importance for the understanding of schizophrenia. Schizophrenic patients have a marked sensitivity to what is going on mentally in other individuals. They respond to minute clues signaled to them by others (the therapist included) while ignoring overt verbal communication.

In every one an innate biological signal code exists, also called 'archaic sign code,' which has a tremendous communicative impact. Archaic communication may be defined as a rudimentary remnant of animal signals, originally used as a warning to fellow creatures to flee or hide. In human beings these signals are the manifold signs used for mood conveyance or for transmitting a state of general alarm. We understand many of these signs to be remnants of early infantile, or even intrauterine, behavior[13]. A continual appeal for help may be broadcast through various

78

bodily symptoms. A baby may express an appeal for more coddling through numerous colds. Itching, may be a signal that some inner emotional discharge is about to begin. It may indicate a need for increased affection or constitute a camouflage for sadistic fantasies.

In observing these primary biologic signs we discover the following rules: *The more a human expression approaches an archaic form of communication, the more contagious is the meaning it conveys.*

Some of these archaic signs are appropriate adaptive responses of the fetus, well observed during intrauterine life, such as active rotation, flexion, or a stretching of the body. From the eighth intrauterine week on the embryonic organism lives in a total rhythmic behavior, and reactive and protective movements are noted[12]. Most probably the fetus lives in a rhythmic sound-world filled with auditive impressions from the maternal heart, with a mean frequency of 70, and a different rhythm from its own fetal heart with a mean frequency of 140 superimposed upon it. The fetus is observed also to react to sounds from the outside world[19]. This observation, combined with the knowledge that the amniotic fluid is a better sound conductor than air, makes the acceptance of a prenatal rhythmic sound-world more than probable.

Rhythmic rocking, dancing and floating in the amniotic fluid belong to the well-observed normal intrauterine movements[19]. The child in the uterus yawns, (intrauterine drinking), scratches, and stretches as a response to stimulation from outside. Every mother knows about this lively conduct of her child within.

Some of the other appropriate adaptive responses, which seem later to be so contagious, can be observed immediately after birth. The child shows rhythmic behavior while sucking at the breast immediately after birth. When the first feeding is not delayed beyond a six hour period, the child also shows the pumping reflex with its hands while manipulating mother's breasts, a pawing reflex movement so well known in cats. Usually mother and baby show a common rhythm during the feeding which is repressed after too long a delay of the first nipple searching behavior. The baby also shows a third form of rhythmic movement of the head while going from one breast to the other. The infant pulls back its lips when satisfied (smile), or turns the head away when unwilling to drink (the gesture of 'no'). The newborn coughs and scratches; it shivers from cold. When frustrated in its appropriate foodsearching movements, the child will displace the innate appropriate movements to other objects. Head-banging, *jactatio nocturna*, early masturbation, rhythmic rocking may all be interpreted as manifestations of displaced, appropriate innate reflexes in the service of primary oral gratification.

One of the best known examples of normal archaic communication is the rocking and dancing movement. It is the innate wisdom of every mother that leads her to putting her child to sleep by rhythmic rocking movements. In doing so she is but repeating mnemic impressions of the child when it was floating around in the amniotic fluid in carefree equanimity.

DANCE AND RHYTHM AS PRIMITIVE TOOLS OF COMMUNICATION

The dance is an imitative movement used by primitive man, by means of which he imitates animals as a magic defense against them. The imitation makes people feel magically stronger than the animal and thus they wrest control from the animals by way of magic. Some Indian tribes still believe that the dance is taught to them by animals. It would lead us too far afield to describe how much dance and rhythm are used in the animal kingdom to transmit messages to other animals, as we see, for example in bees and in the mating dances of higher animals. For our purpose we may state, however, that in man the dance inadvertently brings to life vague reminiscences of archaic rhythmic movements and of the nirvanic existence before birth. In early religious experience dance and magic gesture helped indeed to establish communal participation, that is to say, communion of the various individual members.

It is important to be aware of the contagiousness and the empathy-provoking action of archaic signs and expressions. In observing these early biologic responses everybody inadvertently takes part in the process. The listener may feel an itching sensation when, for instance, the subjects of scratching or skin-touching are brought up in the course of a conversation. Many people cannot see skin diseases without becoming itchy themselves. So again: *the closer a human expression approaches an archaic form of communication, the more unobtrusive is the communicative meaning it conveys.* Mental contagion is the result of a common back - ward pull, a mutual pushing of people into reminiscence, regression, and infantilism.

Laughing, crying, yawning, stretching, shivering, shuddering, and scratching may directly and immediately evoke similar responses in others. The same contagious action is true for running, speeding, clapping hands, rhythmic cheering – all inadvertent reminiscences of the infantile drive for immediate and direct gratification, or reminiscences of the so contagious flight reactions to fear.

Something occurs in people during observation of such archaic sign behavior. An inner resonance unwittingly pushes them back into their own childhood memories. The shared regressive fantasy provokes a deep inner resonance and may lead to a direct identification and empathy with others.

The factor of common regression and unconscious identification through archaic signs and gestures, or through the hypnotic drive of words has been exploited in political strategy, where full use is made of its contagious action. Uniforms, flags, rhythmic marching, communal singing, ritual gestures (Nazi salute) turn people – and especially youth – more easily into mechanically acting, conforming automatons. Rhythmic sloganizing brought entire populations into hypnotic ecstasy: 'Duce, Duce, Duce!' – 'Sieg Heil, Sieg Heil!'

Just as all of us are contagiously affected by yawning – which in itself may be explained as a remnant of fetal drinking and a sign of yearning for food and sleep – so do we find other archaic signs easily leading to mental contagion and shared primitive identification. The same compulsive imitation in others can be brought about by staring, gazing, mimicking and grimacing. Pantomime and imitation of a public figure or an actor suggest that other people unconsciously do the same.

The universal communion of archaic movements is a principal factor in the concept of mental contagion. Because of this communion people are compelled to imitate what others act out for them.

Gestural contagion can be observed in religious ecstatic revivals. Some sects produce a ritual of archaic movements leading to easier communion and participation in their special beliefs – as for instance the sects of the Jumpers and Shakers did in Pennsylvania in the beginning of the nineteenth century. The rhythm of swaying movements during prayer also induces this communion of feelings. It is the contagion of movement, or shuddering and shivering and the common expectation of salvation that leads into the common ecstatic experience of the *mysterium tremendum*. In people who have survived a catastrophe, such as bombing or confinement in a concentration camp, I have observed comparable signs of automatic, imitative behavior. The more completely they had lost their own feeling of identity the more readily they imitated the gestural signs of others. Back in normal circumstances they lost this over-all identifying behavior very soon.

THE UNOBTRUSIVE SUBMISSION
TO SOCIAL PATTERNS

The intricate, subtle observations during group therapy have taught us how the participants, without knowing they are doing it, unobstrusively take over from one another special habits and patterns of behavior. They take over as well as repudiate. But even while criticizing one another something sifts and leaks through the mental barrier of their criticism and inner defenses, consequently they are forced to follow the slow coercion of the stronger personality. In the group the critical barrier against suggestions and fascination is rather weak.

Psychologically we may interpret much of man's identifying behavior as a search for anonymity, a protective, magic need to be inconspicuous. We can compare this with camouflage in the animal kingdom. 'When I am anonymous and inconspicuous, nothing can happen to me. 'The same is true, for instance, for a well-known reaction to danger called 'freezing' or being 'petrified with fright.' We find this sham-death attitude (also called catalepsy) as a form of mimicry and camouflage in moments of danger throughout the entire animal kingdom[16]. Nothing is as contagious as this fear catalepsy. During the Second World War I repeatedly saw how people in so-called shock (catalepsy-death-attitude) surrendered themselves passively to the very danger they dreaded[17]. By their death-like behavior they aroused in the bystanders even greater fear than the actual bombing or destruction. The same contagious action is repeatedly observed from the extremely infectious and physiologically comparable fainting spell.

The wave of panic in a crowd spreads swiftly, as if a direct telepathic communication existed between one panicky person and the other. In a study on panics I could relate the experience in a London shelter during World War II, where a silent panic caused cataleptic death in several individuals[17]. Hypnotic catalepsy, the trance produced by quacks on the stage, also incites a most contagious identification.

Yet, by thinking only in terms of pathology we are wrong. Inadvertently people imitate each other. Child behaves like his parent, student like his teacher, patient like his therapist. An unobtrusive mental contagion is going on the world over, because man is a communal animal, eagerly trying to be 'at home' in a group and to identify with it.

MENTAL POLLUTION

Apathy, rigidity, collective feeling of paralysis and fear are highly contagious feelings. They provoke passive 'frozen' attitudes in nearly everyone. After natural catastrophies and war we may experience such a collective mental paralysis. We see this, for instance, in primitive tribes who, paralyzed by hunger, become more and more passive and apathetic and finally sur-

83

render to famine and death, even when food turned out to be not far away[21]. Mental epidemics are nearly always connected with fear, exhaustion, and famine, causing apathy and inertia, providing a fertile ground for deluded thinking. Isolation and the frustration resulting from it through lack of communication can have the same effect.

Various religious sects practice fasting and systematic bodily exhaustion intentionally to induce a state of greater mental receptivity in their followers. Asceticism furthers the formation of hallucinations, while mass asceticism paves the way to mental mass contagion and delusion.

Sophistication and literacy do not protect people against mental contagion. Simple literacy often promotes conformism, while mere sophistication without emotional maturity makes people more receptive to intellectualized suggestions. It is not difficult to cause mass contagion even among sophisticated people. During a festive cruise it is only necessary to call 'shipwreck' to cause collective hallucinations of drowning and wrecks. On troopships during the anxious tension of war we had to deal daily with mass hallucinations of discovery of hostile 'U' boats. Since the Sputniks went into the air, the mirages of mysterious flying saucers from outer space have increased again.

Collective psychoses were already clearly observed by Greek and Romans. We have the examples of the mystery cults whose members assumed various ecstatic attitudes climaxing in epileptic convulsions. The Greeks sometimes referred to those convulsions as contagious satyrdelusions.

Especially the rites of public dance and revival restores the magic realm of infancy, the return to a blessed state that has passed. In the mass, where one's anonymity is preserved, unconscious drives are more easily discharged and the feeling of merging, of equalization and mutual participation is enhanced.

At present we have the contagious rhythmic spread and expansion of Rock and Roll, already on the wane. The dance is of tremendous importance as a simultaneously binding and freeing element for coincidental and casual groups. Rhythm brings them together in a collective archaic dream as did the St. Vitus Dance in the Middle Ages.

Modern St. Vitus Dance has assumed various aspects. Collective fear still evokes the same restless movements among people. Modern man tries to escape his stress in the raving frenzy of automobiles and airplanes. Jazz, Rock and Roll, and other rhythms lure people to archaic depths while becoming part of a rhythmic mass of sound and movement.

A rhythmical call to a crowd easily foments mass ecstacy. Such provocation of archaic images is used in the strategy of every dictator. Rhythmic chant and rhyme have a coercive action on our civilization, as we can, for instance, observe in the seductive use of jingles in radio advertising. For hours and hours people cannot rid themselves of these jingles and unconsciously they hum with it the praise of the commercial product.

Certain archaic emotional movements can be very easily suggested to the masses, as for instance, tapping, clapping, tom-tom playing.

Sometimes mental mass contagion acquires a strange suicidal aspect as we observe in times of revolution. Romantic daring and audacious heroism may be chosen as a means of inconspicuous self-destruction and self-punishment. It is as if the mass simultaneously fears and loves the excitement of panic and explosion. Some even long masochistically for slavery. People in fear and panic do not like freedom. At such moments the receptivity to mental contagion and the submissiveness of the masses are greater than is usually supposed. Strangely enough it is Hitler who emphasized this collective submissiveness – the *Hingabe Bereitschaft* of the masses.

PROTECTION AGAINST MENTAL CONTAGION

Strength to withstand mental infection and psychic contagion is acquired through the utmost freedom in the exchange of ideas, which produces mature, self-assertive human beings, able to check their sensitivity towards archaic exchanges of feelings.

Wherever there is communicative frustration mental contagion breaks through more readily.

Of clinical importance is the question how to increase the persuasion-resistance of the individual. Hunger, defective intelligence and racial and cultural habits may make for greater persuasive vulnerability. The fact is that mere mechanical sophistication, through which individuals get lost in facts and ideologies, makes these people more vulnerable to mental infection and coercive techniques than those lacking such confusing sophistication.

Somatic infections do not stay on one side of a frontier, neither does mental infection. The more an international community will accept the concept of mental infection and its inherent dangers, the more it will have to establish rules to prevent such form of aggressive contagion. Yet, several 'sacred' international principles will have to be overhauled. Nobody is, for instance 'diplomatically' permitted even to criticize internal events of another state. This is called interference with another state's 'sacred' autonomy. However, the notion that some sacred autonomies can be looked at as sources of dangerous mental infection will finally urge the international community to formulate rules and laws to prevent such mental contagion. But it will take a long time before the world is mature enough to allow such mutual interference.

To correct contagious mass delusion and mental infection is one of the most difficult tasks of a free world founded on an International Charter of Human Rights. Mutual influence and persuasion are continually going on and do not recognize frontiers and iron curtains. Democracy pleads for freedom of thought and this means that it demands the right of all men to test all forms of collective emotion and collective thinking. To preserve this right, however, democracy must face the task of remaining alert and open-minded in order to keep itself free from blind fears and the impact of mental coercion and contagion.

Mental infection may be defined as the existence of a pathogenic inductor spreading pathogenic suggestions. Man, looked at as standing in the center of a web of manifold communications, will unobtrusively be pushed into a regressive form of empathy and sign acceptance whenever he perceives archaic sign-communication in his fellow-beings.

The innate signal code which seduces people into common regression is rather simple: fetal responses, rhythmic and infantile gestures play a principal role in this empathy-provoking behavior. Thus mental contagion may be redefined according to its dynamics as a common backward pull or a mental pushing of people into reminiscence, regression and infantilism.

Attention is asked for the growing danger of mental infection in a society where the technical means of communication have grown beyond the critical selective barriers of the individual psyche.

BIBLIOGRAPHY

1. AZIMA, H. and CRAMER-AZIMA, F.J., 'Studies on Perceptual Isolation,' Dis. Nerv. System, Monogr. Supplement, July, 1957.
2. BOLK, L., 'On the Problem of Anthropogenesis,' Proceedings, Royal Academy of Science, Amsterdam, 1925.
3. CHRISTOFFEL, H., 'Gähnen and Sich-Dehnen,' Schw. Med. Wschr., 1951.
4. CHRISTOFFEL, H., 'Trieb und Kultur,' Basel: Schwabe Verlag, 1944.
5. Conference on Group Processes (No. III), Josiah Macy, Jr., Foundation, New York, 1957.
6. CRITCHLEY, M., The Language of Gesture, Arnold, London, 1939.
7. DARWIN, C., The Expression of the Emotions in Man and Animals, (London, 1890. New York, 1955.
8. EHRENWALD, J., New Dimensions of Deep Analysis. Allen and Unwin, London, 1954.
9. FITZHERBERT, J., 'Some Further Observations on Headbumping and Allied Behavior,' J. Ment. Sci. Vol. 98, 1952.
10. GRALNICK, A., 'Folie a Deux, a Review of 100 cases,' Psychiat, Quart., 1942.
11. GRUENBERG, E.M., 'The Epidemiology of Mental Disease,' Scientific American, March, 1954.
12. HOOKER, D., The Prenatal Origin of Behavior, Univ. of Kansas Press, 1952.
13. MEERLOO, J.A.M., 'Archaic Behavior and the Communicative Act,' Psych. Quart. Vol. 29, 1955.
14. MEERLOO, J.A.M., Communication and Conversation, International Univ. Press, New York, 1950.
15. MEERLOO, J.A.M., Delusion and Mass-Delusion, Nervous and Ment. Dis. Monog. New York, 1949.

16. MEERLOO, J.A.M., 'Human Camouflage and Identification with the Environment' Psychosomatic Medicine, Vol. 19, 1957.
17. MEERLOO, J.A.M., Patterns of Panic, International Univ. Press, New York, 1948.
18. MEERLOO, J.A.M., 'Fear and the Flu,' The New Leader, January 6, 1958.
19. MINKOWSKI, M., 'Neurobiologische Studien am Menschlichen Foetus,' Hdbuch Biol. Arbeitsmethodien, Bd. 5, 1928.
20. SOLOMON, P. et al., 'Sensory Deprivation'. Am. J. Psychiatr. Vol. 114, 1957.
21. SCHWEITZER, A., Experiences in Lambarene (Dutch Edition) Haarlem, 1925.
22. THORNE, F.G., 'Epidemological Studies of Chronic Frustration – Hostility – Aggression States,' Amer. J. Psychiatr., Vol. 113, 1957.
23. TOLSMA, F.J., 'Modern Psychiatric Views on the Induced Psychosis,' Folia Psychiatrica Neerlandica, Vol. 54, 1951.

6. Rock 'n Roll: A Modern Aspect of St. Vitus Dance

IMPLICATIONS FOR THE THEORY
OF MENTAL CONTAGION

The first time I witnessed the spontaneous outburst of the rhythmic ritual of Rock 'n Roll was in a small town. Here, in a combination of drugstore and diner, a juke-box sent forth a seductive rhythm supported by a whining set of sounds. From the very first note the young people near the small bar were irrepressible. They started to dance, – no, that is hardly the right word. A frenzied rhythmic seizure took possession of them; they yelled and shouted and rocked themselves more and more into a rhythmic trance until it had gone far beyond the accepted versions of human dancing.

Before the music had started the place had been the usual, rather dull, meeting place full of the concentrated boredom and frustration of a Sunday afternoon. The local people go to such 'joints' to see each other, to sip highballs and to gossip about others. The casual stranger feels the frustration, the tiredness of the mind that cannot find a conversation worth pursuing – boy looks at girl and does not know what to feel or even what to want. He sips his drink and becomes still more silent. Then the juke-box fills the awkward silence with melodramatic noise. Suddenly, as if by magic, the quivering rhythm gets hold of the teenagers and drags them from their high perches at the counter. The music brings to life an old- age-old complaint, a nagging melody. It is the crying and crooning and hopeless sorrow of a deprived mankind aroused by the pouting and self-pity we feel for ourselves. The forgotten and rejected baby in people – because they had to grow up – awakens and pants for new satisfaction, for new rocking and endearment. Negro-blues and cow-boy songs and jazzy rhythms are united in seductive rocking, appealing to unconscious tendencies in man. Here we have no singing, but rather gasping and sobbing, snivelling and blubbering. There is squealing and whimpering, whining and yelping, writhing, rocking and rolling, aroused by a torturous rhythmic monotony.

OUT OF THIS WORLD

From now on the rocking people temporarily forget their boring civilization, and prehistoric man in them comes to life. A wild pantomime is displayed resembling the rhythm of tribal utterances and the ritual trance and convulsive outcry of revivals. No, this is no music, and no plain unadulterated sex, as some authors claim, but only suggestive contagious rhythm. It is being energized by the excitement of one's own body rhythms and by the desperate ecstasy that wants to throw away control. This is a way of mobilizing the epinephrine in one's system, – jazz and the 'hoop' achieve the same result.
True, it is also an outburst of sexual rhythm of the pelvis without real erotic fulfillment, and with aimless shaking of the hips. The youngsters keep even more distance than in usual dancing. It is the exalted trance of a dream without reality; it is an outlet, an act of excited, common frustration without joyful rapture.

THE COVER-UP

The glamorous show of ecstatic abandon may cover up the empty feeling of something lacking deep within people. It is the incoherent expression of the fantasy of living in a love-lorn world. It is a sleepdancing and mass-hypnotism, a collective trance. It is boredom and frustration concentrated into a rhythmic trance of the body, while the mind goes dead. Awareness is gone, personality is gone, most of the sense of shame is gone. Everything is permitted in this orgy of rhythm and music. In the rocking trance man is as if drunk – dance drunk. He may attack, he may foam with rage, he may yell, he may destroy, he may even use the vulgar sexual movements that are taboo – civilized restraint is abandoned, but never completely.

A new kind of hero is worshipped all over the world, – the tough kid, the hostile baby in us living in a desperate state of continual repressed temper tantrum. Another hero is the suicidal maniac of speed in his sports car. The upset movie actor, who died not long ago in his sportscar in a raving frenzy, may clinically be considered as possessed by the same murderous and suicidal tendency as primitive man running amok. Yet his death led to a cult of adoration in many a 'Weltschmerzed' teenager.

The archaic rhythm of the tom-tom or Rock 'n Roll leads the adolescents, warmed up by jazz, to a common regression, and back to the state of common hypnosis initiated by the drum-ritual of prehistoric times. In the ancient rhythmic trance and ritual – the Dionysiac orgies in Greece and the Roman Bacchanalia – people not only grew shameless, but the collective orgiastic dance let them act out what was usually taboo to them. In modern Rock 'n Roll, our youngsters dream and shriek and writhe and twist themselves as if wrestling with all the burden of civilized restraint. True, all this affords a temporary liberation from the pressure of civilization, but it is a rebellion without the progressive, ideational means. The dancers become a mass of unarticulated form, – stammering, sweating and salivating in this new version of archaic singsong and unsublimated gesture of sex. The whining and stammering for love and tenderness is a disguise for raging inner feelings of deprivation; it is the same disguise we so often find in mental depressive states.

CATHARSIS IN C

On the more positive side, however, the monotonous repetition of gestures releases tension and also acquires the function of conquering some inner conflict combined with it. A guided dance mania can have cathartic and sublimating action, though this may be completely out of the awareness of the dancers themselves. Usually we see that the dance epidemic runs its own course and dies out.

The contagious rhythm of Rock 'n Roll swept the country as a form of mass-hypnosis; it went around the whole world, we may say, and through its nearly hypnotic fascination it got out of hand in many places. From a demonstration dance it sometimes became a destructive fury and open rebellion of temporarily anesthetized teenagers. Swept on by a tremendous money-making potential of those who make the musical records, it demonstrated the violent mayhem long repressed everywhere on earth. Of course, the record-making companies feel no particular concern for the poisonous mental contagion they may spread.

PSYCHOLOGIC QUESTIONS

The example of the tremendous mental contagiousness of Rock 'n Roll and related mass-phenomena (the 'hoop' and 'beetle'-mania went around the world faster than the Asian Flu) arouses several psychologic questions. For instance, what will it do mentally to the afflicted youth? Is it a bad manifestation? Will it foster more juvenile delinquency? Can we allow people to exploit the expressive sensitivity of our teenagers? Happily enough we are aware that through all history mankind has known these frenzied outbursts of those in despair as well as in ebullient joy, which did not corrupt youth after all.

This, however, does not imply that we should not seek better to understand and prevent such unpredictable forms of mass-hysteria which may easily get out of hand. Too much mass-excitement is incompatible with individual ego development and becoming a personality. We had better look toward means of supplanting it and leading it into useful channels.

In this chapter I want especially to look at this new aspect of the age-old St. Vitus Dance as an example of a nearly unexplored chapter of psychology – that of mental contagion.

Every repetitious rite and inculcated habit pattern unwittingly drags man's memory back to the period of conditioning in infancy, the period in which gestures and actions were learned in a redundant and monotonous way. The cheer of a football club, the ritualistic salute of a political group, and many other social rites also signify some secret longing for the magic dream-country of the baby, for return to a bygone blessed state of simple redundant gestural contact with fellow beings. In the mass, however, where one's anonymity is more easily preserved, people are better able to get rid of daily frustrations, and suppressed inner drives are more quickly discharged. The cult, the rites, the music, the ceremonial are merely justification for this deeper need for regression to a less civilized state. Token forms of such temporary regressions may be observed at a masked ball or at a carnival, where the mask and the anonymity facilitate less restrained behavior.

The mass epidemic of dance fury after World War I is fresh in my memory. The same phenomenon could be witnessed during and after World War II. It is as if collective tension and anxiety become partially freed and alleviated in such rhythmic endeavor. Dance and rhythm are of tremendous importance as a simultaneously binding and freeing element in the group. Through dance and orgiastic behavior primitive tribes try to escape their fear of the tribal gods.

In the first century, Plutarch described such a dance epidemic among the girls of Milete. When rumors of the Black Death (plague) reached the girls, they burst into furious dancing and showed all kinds of ecstatic attitudes and several finally committed suicide. The therapy for this behavior was curious. When these girls were threatened with being dragged naked through the streets, dead or alive, the mass-psychosis disappeared.

Toward the end of the fourteenth century several contagious epidemics of dance fury swept Germany and spread to all of Europe. This so-called St. Vitus Dance (also named Chorea

Major) followed famine and the Black Plague. The victims of the epidemic broke into dancing and were unable to stop. Even cloisters were infected with this 'chorea Germanicorum,' as it was called then. In Italy the same process was referred to as 'Tarantism' and was explained as the result of a toxic bite by a spider, the tarantula.

SEEING IS INVOLVING

Even the observation of an exalted dance casts a mysterious spell on people. The spectators too are gradually carried away by the rhythmic ecstasy. They are compelled to join. The children's crusades and the tale of the Pied Piper of Hamelin reminds us of these seductive, contagious dance furies. The children of the crusade went dancing to the Holy Land to fight the Barbarians. The story runs that most of them starved and died, or were finally sold as slaves.

History records many similar motile mass-psychoses as reaction to war, fear, and persecution. Toward the end of the sixteenth century, the period of reformation and religious persecution, a comparable mass reaction is reported among children. Following a dance, these children assumed the delusion that they were cats. They climbed trees and began to meow. Driven by mass-contagion they had lost their personal identity.

The modern St. Vitus dance has assumed a different aspect. Latent fear and frustration still evoke restless movement among people. Modern man tries to escape his fears in the raving frenzy of automobiles and airplanes. We may speak of a true chorea of the highway. When, however, the man does not have a thrilling car, why not fall back on the old pattern of a dancing trance near a jazz-band or a juke-box? Modern man is not able to relax alone and by himself, but feels driven to be on a constant lookout for company, movement, amusement and diversion. Jazz and other rhythms lure people, and especially youth, to archaic psychic depths so that they may become part of, and feel they belong to a chaotic mass of sound and movement. Constant movement and intoxication turn people into wild dancing children.

94

A rhythmical call to the crowd easily foments mass ecstasy, as we experienced in the contagious, cheery catchwords of dictatorships: 'Sieg Heil, Sieg Heil,' or 'Duce, Duce, Duce!' The call repeats itself into the infinite and liberates the mind of all reasonable inhibitions. Become a follower of Rock 'n Roll and, as in drug-addiction, a thousand years of civilization fall away in a single moment.

The psychologic answer is rather simple. Rhythm is the first sensual experience, engulfing people even before they are born. The child in its mother's womb lives in a totally rhythmic world. The auditive sense is ready for function and it hears mother's heartbeat as well as its own in a syncopated two-to-one harmony (mother's heartbeat 70, the child's 140). The unconscious organic memory and mnemonic experience of this nirvana and fully-protected existence remains in everybody. Every mother makes use of this innate wisdom; she repeats the rhythm and rocks her baby to sleep. Every musical rhythm awakens memories unobtrusively from our infantile past and may arouse a deep yearning and homesickness.

There are various early infantile habits and movements which are easily aroused in people by seeing them happen in others. Especially the so-called archaic movements and signs which were originally appropriate adaptive reflexes are empathy-provoking. Coughing, laughter, crying, yawning, itching, scratching, shivering, rocking – all these produce the same inadvertent actions in fellow beings. The one who scratches arouses feelings of itching in the other. The one who yawns makes those near him feel like yawning. We may express this in the following psychologic law: *The more a human expression reminds people of the infantile (and even intrauterine) existence, the more contagious is this expression.* Or, to say it in more sophisticated words: *The more a human expression represents an archaic reflex and adaptation, the more unobtrusive is the communicative meaning it conveys.*

Rock 'n Roll, even dancing itself, or the witnessing of such rhythmic or archaic regressive behavior, push and drag people, in spite of themselves, back into their infantile reminiscences as do music, sounds and smells. The common regressive fantasy, provoked by rhythm and hot jazz, arouses in people a deep inner resonance and incites them to join in the common orgy of exalted anonymity. The crying and crooning activities, the self-pity and passivity forced on people by our technical era tend to make Rock 'n Roll an exciting outlet. Mass-psychologic in effect, it points up how deep is the latent fear in man and the urge in people to regress and forget.

This craze will pass as have all other paroxysms of exciting dance mania. Important in the situation, however, is our notion that there exists an ultrasensitive mood conveyance, and that there are so many resounding chords in modern youth ready to act when the seductive rhythms are in the air. These may easily become the signs of breaking down of values because of a lack of a strong controlling force inside the psyche. In a technologic world, where the easy luxury of gadgets smothers the growth of true personality and mechanical communication is a million-fold more effective, easy mental contagion becomes more and more a danger. A perpetual Rock 'n Roll is only one of the signs of such de-personalization of the individual and of the ecstatic veneration of mental passivity.

If people cannot stem and control this strange tide with its waves of rhythmic narcosis and vicarious craze, it could be that people are again preparing their downfall in the midst of pandemic funeral dances. The dance pandemics of the Middle Ages occurred not so long ago in history. Let us hope that mankind does not need the dance-craze any more – this infantile outlet – to give vent to, and to overcome the deep-seated anxieties aroused by the technical and atomic revolution.

7. Responsibility and Normality

A PSYCHOLINGUISTIC INVESTIGATION

INTRODUCTION

The word *responsibility*, the subject of my research, is used by different people with various meanings and intentions. At one pole it is a behavioristic term and, as such, lends itself to clinical investigation; at the other pole, it is a value expressing ideal behavior. But because of its normative content it is dependent on and related to various cultural and social evaluations.

I may call this study a psycholinguistic approach because my emphasis is on the variety of meanings condensed in one and the same word. This kind of operational research has the value of approaching a problem from various angles, thereby increasing the probability that the core of the problem will be grasped. Every understanding is an interpretation created with the tools and means acquired from our cultural past. I am aware that while observing and judging we never completely lose this subjectivity. We are, as it were, always standing in our own way. The word responsibility never covers the concept of responsibility. But different approaches increase the probability that we will cover most of the ground.

THE SEMANTICS OF RESPONSIBILITY

A mother scolded her three-year-old daughter for being irresponsible when the little girl told her a childish fantasy. Yet this fantasy was the child's first *response* to a world of mystery.

97

What a confusion of words we are in already! There are responsibilities we accept with joy and pride; others we evade at any price.

In daily life the word *responsible* is used in such multivarious ways that an investigation of how the word and its synonyms are used places us directly in the midst of psychological involvements. Since the word contains a condensation of the history of its various meanings, the usages of the past reverberate in every expression of the word. This fact justifies the use of psycholinguistic approach.

Responsibility is derived from *spondere*, to speak or to pledge, and with the prefix, *respond* means to speak back and to answer. In order to be responsible one must be able to be the *sponsor* of one's own thoughts. It requires the highest rationality of being able to verbalize and explain the feelings and thoughts that are in one's mind. The word is also related to the French *épouser*, getting married, to speak out who your mate is and to be committed to him or her.

In a social sense, responsibility means being able to give an *answer* to the questions asked (in Dutch, *verantwoorden*). The primitive or the child who is not yet able to speak cannot be responsible. He cannot give account, cannot answer a charge, and therefore is not to be held *answerable* and *accountable*. (In German *jemand anrechnen*). In terms of developmental psychology, the functions of responding, answering and accounting are not yet supposed to be present in early childhood. The act cannot be verified. Sometimes accountability is used in this sense: Should he pay with his life?

Another synonym is *imputability*, from the Latin *imputo* and our word *pure*, making someone responsible for his 'dirty' and guilty act. Here too we detect a psychological developmental root, so well expressed in the Dutch equivalent, *verschoonbaarheid*, meaning this: Is the person able to cleanse himself, to keep the body clean? Originally it also meant cleansed by fire through divine ordeal, purged from being putrid. Our words imputation and reputation have the same root. Imputability now has the meaning: Can the person be legally punished or revenged? What is his guilt and *culpability?* Is there awareness of the imputable act? Are the acts he did *amendable? Amendability* and *amenability* are expressions for responsibility more frequently used in Great Britain. They show the root *mend*, the ability to better and repair the omission or the faulty deed, though they express a more general meaning of being under the law. Amends are the compensations and satisfactions one gives to those hurt. An older derivation is from the Latin *minari*, to threaten and the ability to be led. Amenable means to be easily led, and is related to our word *demeanor*. In trying to judge someone's responsibility, the problem of how he can be led and influenced unwittingly plays an important role.

From an economic standpoint one arrives at the question of a man's *standing surety* (for debts), *liability* and *reliability;* somebody is apt to be asked account for; he incurred a responsibility or obligation. Liability itself is derived from the Latin *ligare* and *religare,* being bound to group and faith, and thus unwittingly has a religious undercurrent. Liable means liable to group values, but also guilt and culpability and being, liable to penalty – in German, *Haftbarkeit.*

All this responsibility can be disclaimed by the person in question; he denies and negates the social relation and obligation by 'not responding,' not giving account, by pretending not to be aware or by truly being *non compos mentis.*

The latter question of mental competence during an act or during the period of judgment and trial came into play much later in history. Even today there is much confusion when, in a criminal case, for instance, the question of mental competence and responsibility is asked of the expert. What must one judge – the intention of the act, the culpability of the person, the suffering of the victim, the vulnerability and vengefulness of the social formation, the psychological structure of the incriminated person, the possible re-education of the criminal drive?

This paper aims to give a survey of the variations of the concept of responsibility in the hope of making the reader more familiar with the subtle pitfalls of the concept. Usually the reliability of a man – criminal or author – is judged by the capacity to control himself, his capacity to conform to the group and his consistency in behavior. Even a writer has to take responsibility for his way of communication. Is he able to outgrow his professional jargon for the sake of greater clarity? Does he dare to show his own commitments without retreat to the usual quotation compulsion? He is also responsible for the timing of his communication; he can be too early or too late with his ponderings.

THE VARIATIONS OF RESPONSIBILITY

The divisions I outline here – some of which will overlap each other – are only few of many others that could be imagined, but they lead us immediately into the manifold difficulties caused by the careless use of the concept of responsibility.

Responsibility for action. This implies that man is a freeacting moral agent, without taking into account the various unconscious conditioning incentives that may short-circuit him into actions even against himself. Much of man's judgment about freedom of action depends on his conscious or unaware thinking about the problem of causality and indeterminacy.

According to epistemology there exists an innate indeterminacy not due to the inadequacy of man's existing knowledge but related to the fact that every observer of phenomena stands in his own way while observing and evaluating, especially when he judges special microphysical dimensions and subtleties. The various goals and tendencies active in a person – some overt, some hidden or even more deeply repressed – make for indeterminate prediction of his actions.

Man's rigid need for causality can be divided into a need to get away from inferences and observational prejudices, and a magic *explanation-mania* steeped in infantile thought of omnipotence and fear of the unknown.

The psychological problem of freedom of action or determinacy has acquired new aspects since, clinically, we discovered that many a young person acts out what his parents unconsciously want him to do, though they repress the act in themselves. That is why the law, though disregarding this intimate relation, often makes parents responsible for the acts of their children. In the annals of jurisprudence there are murders known to have been committed in hypnotic trance, and consequently the suggestor was punished and not the hypnotized person. In youthful criminality the suggestive influence of the gangleader and mastermind is an important determinant.

In a psychological way, we may say that freedom is the way our unique identity has an impact on our experiences. Freedom is the risk of our own individuality. It is the indeterminacy in the potentialities we make use of. It is the difference between what is done and what can be done.

Responsibility for action means accepting the consequences of one's action, even though failure may be involved. Yet there is a common human tendency to make the other fellow more responsible for one's failures than for one's successes. Praise and acknowledgment are difficult human gifts.

There also exists a *delusion of responsibility* in people who want to be over-responsible and who want to have their fingers in every pie. These are the narcissistic individuals who are never able to delegate responsibility. Their search for acknowledgment and status denies a self-assertive identity to other people.

A *precocious responsibility* is often heaped by parents on the oldest child, whom they want to take part in the moral education of the younger siblings. I have seen great conflicts growing out of this denial of natural sibling rivalry. The precocious overburdening with moral values often leads to a flight into a persistent irresponsibility.

Quarreling parents often forget that they make their child feel responsible for their disharmonious behavior.

Responsibility for omission. The above analysis leads us also to accept responsibility for negative action. Non-action is also action; non-treatment is also treatment. There exists a contamination with paralysis, a corruption by prudency and a betrayal through evasion.

In education we recognize what a responsibility, for instance, a dominating, sarcastic mother has who does not feel and show respect for her husband and thus does not help the child in building up respect for authority. Parents can dominate the child through omission of good examples, through contaminating the child with their doubts and quarrels, or they can burden the child with precocious responsibility, which so often occurs when one of the parents dies early. Most ominous is when the child is made responsible too early for the emotions he arouses in the parent: 'Look, what you are doing to me!'

Man's inner conscience feels especially responsible for the omission of charitable actions. Much mourning and selfreproach is based on this awareness of neglect and omission.

Responsibility for one's thinking. An old Dutch proverb says, 'Thoughts are toll-free,' meaning, 'think what you will, lest you do not express it.' This saying goes out from the naive belief that there exists a vacuum between thinking people that can be bridged *only* by spoken communication. But already man's gestures transmit part of his thinking. So do his hostilities and friendships besides many other subtle clues that take part in man's intercommunication.

Suspicion as expressed in paranoiac thinking is especially contagious. It usually does not contradict logic, and very easily arouses the same paranoiac thinking in other people.

There are many people who have been punished and ostracized – especially by rebellious mobs – for gestures that were interpreted as representing subversive thinking.

In totalitarian regimes the tyrant is not content with winning submission of the body but also requires meekness of spirit. Yet, taking a stand and pledging adherence on the basis of know-nothing is also a habit in democratic regimes. The tyrant with his system of thought control is continually on the lookout not only for rebellious action but also for unspoken rebellious thoughts. The pokerfaced gestural insubordination was heavily punished in Nazi concentration camps; the victims had to show meek submission even facially.

Mutual control of the other fellow's hidden thinking exists and is part and parcel of man's psychological equipment. In various ethical and religious systems, the hostile or blasphemous thought is judged as being sinful. Especially in Western cultures, in which we find a greater sense of guilt and repression than in the Orient, people are made to feel responsible for their unsocial thoughts. The sufferer of phobias and obsessions is continually tortured by his uncontrolled vagrancies of thinking.

Responsibility for feelings. In the period of man's magic thinking he also assumed responsibility for his hidden feelings and thoughts. A child who is angry and has destructive wishes towards one of the parents believes that his anger can be a killing force. Many later, deep-seated feelings of guilt are related to those old repressed murderous fantasies.

The magic interpretation of feelings and thoughts as potent tools can lead to rather paradoxical results. In some tribes, when a man dreams of his wife's infidelity, it is reason for him to divorce her. Though we would now interpret this dream-image as a projection of his wishes onto her, there exists in our own society a cult of suspicion and nearly paranoiac allusion toward other people that burdens them with a deep impact of our own hostile thoughts. Prejudice is usually such a projection of our feelings of inferiority and consequent hostility onto scapegoats and minorities.

Snobbishness and feelings of wanting to humiliate someone can defeat a victim without word or action. It is a high ethical attitude to feel responsible for the emotions aroused in others and for the embarrassment induced.

Since the more intensive study of mental contagion and psychic contamination, we are more aware of the mutual influence of feelings. Panic in the one arouses fear in the other. In tension and fear a renunciation of social responsibilities takes place.

Hatred can be a magic wish to annihilate the fellow-being and unwittingly arouse psychic defenses in him. The gangleaders' psychopathy ensnares his innocent members; my melancholy tends to burden others with my woes. In a more complete study of psychic murder, I could show the influence of a husband's deathwishes on a wife, who accepted this verdict by committing suicide.

Nobody is so much aware of the responsibility for feelings as the physician, whose mood and hopes are active elements in every cure.

Responsibility for one's communications. As noted before there is so much inadvertent mutual communication going on, and also a more profound mental contagion and contamination, that emphasizing the responsibility for communication belongs to this investigation.

I am not thinking only of the purely semantic problem and the limitations of our verbal contact, but of the content of man's persuasions, the slant of his communication; the omission of truth in reporting; the daily communication of hate and aggression and anger through our organs of communication, the press, the radio and TV. There is, for instance, a regular, obsessive infecting with fear of atomic doom. The repetitious blaring of spoken messages encourages a mechanization of thought.

Our mechanical age has made destructive inroads into the mutual contact and communication of many a family.

Responsibility for unobtrusive consequences. If a mother fails to provide sufficient food for a child, the child will finally starve and die. If the mother does this out of a ritualistic food faddism, the unobtrusive consequence is the killing of her child.

There exist many of these complex chess-game consequences, in which a person cannot foresee where his initial act will lead. Serving someone a drink is harmless friendliness under usual circumstances, but when the drink is served to a potential addict, it can be dangerous. Nevertheless, this social seduction of alcoholics in treatment continuously goes on.

Television appears to be an innocent pleasure but can lead to apathy and reading-block in some children because this new social peeping habit (often leading to TV addiction) is unwittingly harmful to the family relation and leads to a strange vicious circle of diminished mutual communication.

Comparable examples could be mentioned for the unwitting influence of social institutions. The German S.S. officers I was asked to investigate at the end of World War II had relinquished their personal moral evaluations for those of the institution, the S.S. state.

There exists a *bureaucratization* of responsibility, which depersonalizes the feeling of individual commitment to a task. Institutionalism undermines personal responsibility in exchange for an automatic conformism.

Responsibility and the system of values. Only those can be truly reponsible who give value to the self. This means they do not obey and 'respond' automatically but have the conviction that a self-piloting ego is involved in evaluating the responsible act.

In this system of self-evaluation transferred to the outside world, various parts of the personality collaborate. Value is given to material things, but also to ideas. Value is given to our status and to acknowledgment. Many people live in a continual self-evaluation by proxy, overestimating other people's images of them. Self-devaluation is often the result of hostility towards the family one came forth from.

Manifold social phenomena ask for our emotional investment. Some are purely hedonistic and relativistic and are related to instinctual gratifications, to our interests and likings; others are experienced by people in a more narcissistic way as the only 'right' and 'goodness' that exists. Those values that come from the superego – after having been taken over and absorbed as moral values from educators, society and church – have the tendency to be conceived as absolute norms. People stand up for them and do not want to exchange those values for new values because once during their development these normative values served as a protection against anxiety. There exist values that serve as protection against the instincts, and there are values steeped in the instinctual needs. Values in contrast to facts cannot be studied by inductive methods; they have to be historically deducted and found out by empathy and sympathy.

This may lead to an inner conflict about values. What people want for themselves often is in conflict with the social values and the need of the community. Which are man's true hopes and values and which are artificially implanted into him? Usually the conflict of motivations and values is not known to the person because too easily the process of self-justification creeps in, in order to deny the real motivation. During World War II, I had to investigate several people who refused to do military service on principal ethical grounds. In several of those so pacifistically minded, I found a strong horror of the eventual release of their own destructive aggressiveness.

For our study, it is important to realize that the feeling of responsibility is continually intruded upon by man's value systems. There are those asserting their own values and those who evaluate continually by proxy, asking themselves only what others will think of them. They only want to be praised and prized without giving value. There are others who have no liking for anybody, no interest, no emotional investment in people and the world and will never take any responsibility. We can call these pathological cases but they throw a sharp light on how man's responsibility is continually shaped by his system of values.

Responsibility to one's own moral standards and evaluations. This bears a close relationship to the previous category, but needs elaboration, for the conflict between *individual conscience* and collective moral evaluation is a very subtle daily occurrence. The core of the Nuremberg Trials and the Eichman Trial involves the question of whether individual conscience prevails beyond automatic submission to orders given, when the orders are in conflict with a person's moral principle.

Little forms of self-betrayal occur often in daily life. Imagine being in a small, intimate circle where an absent individual is slandered, as is often done to get rid of surplus hostility. Under such circumstances it is difficult for many people to break away from the temporary collective mood and defend the absentee. A tragic example of this is what happened during the French Revolution to a close friend of Louis XVI. A member of the National Convention, he realized in horror one day that, in the heat of the collective mood, he had voted for the beheading of his former king. He committed suicide.

This giving in to the collective evaluation, out of prudence and safety, is a common act of self-betrayal.

The process of self-corruption and personal myopia is continually going on, especially when people are tired. There exist self-justifications that continually nag things away from our feelings of responsibility. There is the self-righteousness; bigot ry; the infectious defamation of others; the moral contagion of prejudice; the non-acknowledgment of our shames and personal wrongs; the narrowing of our outlook; the weapon of false indignation; the collecting of injustice – 'What are the other fellows doing to me?' – the toleration of immoral actions for so-called strategic reasons. There is the need to simplify complicated issues and to make use of convenient logic out of laziness. Many people call conformity what really is a giving up of any critical moral evaluation.

In the totalitarian state non-conformity is always looked upon as treason.

In general we may say that man is responsible for the example he is to others by his own life. He cannot preach morality without living it.

Responsibility for repressed tendencies. Although the legal profession looks rather doubtfully at the modern psychological concept of unconscious guilt about hidden crimes, in clinical practice we find it one of the most frequent motivations for committing minor crimes and for being irresponsible. The unsocial act and petty crime try to sidetrack the deeper seated hidden feelings of guilt through a continual quest for either punishment or for other forms of self-destructive behavior.

A girl who was expelled from college for petty stealing had a double aim in her unsocial behavior. She wallowed in self-pity because of the great injustice done to her, while on a deeper psychic layer, soothed her guilty oedipal feelings about her father. At the same time, the verdict brought her back home, the real scene of her crime of wanting to steal her father's love from her mother.

Self-destructive behavior and minor crimes are often forms of a wrongly understood self-justice. In therapy we can make use of this paradoxical and self-incriminating form of responsibility. Ontogenetically there exists a magic circle of responsibility, blaming all responsibility to other persons and things, and a mature circle of responsibility searching to find how one's own failures can be corrected.

Paradoxical responsibility. This is partly related to the previous point, but I want especially to emphasize the need in many people to overstress their feelings of responsibility in order to hide opposite hostile feelings. The *word* responsibility is often misused as a justification and exculpation. The parent who says he feels over-responsible for his child and doesn't dare to let the child have his own freedom and selfassertive behavior, unwittingly brings hidden ambivalences into play. His great responsibility keeps something contrasting under reserve. It is overdoing the controls under the justification of responsibility but actually because of a defiance against letting someone else develop his own responsibility. The hostile part of the human relation is overcontrolled and misused in order to free one's self of eventual remorse and guilty involvement in case some accident should happen. It is at the same time a denial of the law of trial and error.

A special form of the paradoxical responsibility is *culpable neglect* in people who diminish their controls by, for instance, drinking or taking dope. While an alcoholic driver once was judged less liable to punishment if he had caused an accident, most courts would now judge him more culpable.

The responsibility of the drunk leads us into various clinical difficulties. One alcoholic is different from another. One cannot take one aspect out of the total personality in order to judge him, nor can we separate these qualities from the influences of the environment. Some people are pushed into inebriety intentionally in order to make themselves more courageous; other people take to drink and – so they think – are legally less responsible, although the crime was prepared with a cool mind.

Take the assault on a rival out of jealousy. The jealousy of one man can be very different from the jealousy of another. In one, it can be merely a feeling of amorous inferiority; in another, a violent protection against deeply hidden homosexuality.

Many paradoxical forms of responsibility are related to the variety of conscious and unconscious motivations. Man can do the right act for the wrong reasons and the wrong act for the right reasons.

Legal responsibility. Legal responsibility is related to the age of the person, the mentality of the person and the mentality of the social formation. It was not so long ago that a five-year-old girl who stole a loaf of bread was punished with five years in prison. Only total unawareness – like a 'wilde beaste' – could excuse a man from criminal guilt until the establishment in 1845 of the McNaghten Rule. In the Middle Ages even the biological 'wilde beaste' was held responsible and convicted accordingly.

The insanity of McNaghten, who had tried to assassinate the British Prime Minister, led to the rule in British courts that no man can be convicted of a crime who 'was laboring under such defect of reason as not to know the nature or quality of the act he was doing or not to know that the act was wrong.' This rule, now accepted in most of the United States, distinguishes between insane psychotics and other criminals because punishment would have no rational impact on them nor be a salutary example for other potential criminals.

Later the doctrine was added that an 'irresistible impulse' had to be proven (1929 Court of Appeals, Smith vs. the United States) so that the mentally diseased is 'impelled to act by a power which overcame his reason and judgment and to him was irresistible.' The court accepted the existence of such a criminal 'malgré lui,' an urge the law cannot impute.

Important for our investigation is the fact that inadvertently it is accepted that this 'irresistible impulse' comes only from inside a person's mind and never from without. Yet, psychologically, we are aware that seduction to crime does exist – as, for instance in psychosis à deux – and that in its ulterior form, crime can also occur as a form of coercion by individual hypnosis or mass-suggestion. Though the law makes only the person *accountable*, our operational analysis shows that he can be the center of many coercive influences, some more responsible than he.

The Durham Decision in 1954 by the District of Columbia Court of Appeals allowed a plea of insanity if the existence of a mental disease could be demonstrated and if the incriminated act was a product of (or related to) that disease. The problem of psychological excuse for the act gradually became an involved problem related to the question as to what was insanity and what, 'irresistible impulse.' But still omitted is this question: Which are the responsible factors in both the accused and his environment leading to the incriminated act? Society does not like to accuse itself. A tolerant wife who has been nagged day in and day out for years by an irresponsible husband, and who at last explodes with an 'irresistible impulse,' cannot plead insanity, though the real responsibility lies with the husband who provoked the aggression. The maladjustment can either be in the person or in his environment. Usually these responsibilities are interrelated.

At this moment the law supposes too much that antisocial and irresponsible acts are the product of mental disease. Mostly they are not. As a 'friend of the court,' the psychiatrist can only give a survey of various motives and failing responsibilities, that is, of inner dynamics and outer provocations that led to the act. The expert must free himself as much as possible from rigid nomenclature: insanity, psychopathy and mental derangement. There is no simple diagnostic label but only an extensive case history. Several new responsibilities now come into play. The court must work for prevention of the criminal act, but also must take responsibility for the unwitting need of society to revenge and punish the act. Can punishment, the *imputation*, change and cleanse the man?

The more people are only vaguely aware of their own nearly irresistible impulses, the more need they feel to revenge these impulses in others. All people – judge, jury and psychiatrist included – are potential offenders. That is what makes objectivity so difficult. The law is not morality. The law is never self-reflexive about remorse, guilt or satisfaction about actions; only individuals are.

Finally, the accused has to be re-educated or, when there is mental disturbance, to be treated. Only in case of childcriminality is one better aware now of the fact that the environmental factors that provoked the act must also be treated and changed. When, after punishment, a convict is sent back to the same seductive and coercive social influences, new irresponsible acts will follow the more easily.

Responsibility and commitment. There is a great difference between a compulsive commitment on the basis of outside rearing and taming, and a commitment based on inner moral and ethical awareness.

Discipline in children makes for later responsibility and commitment, provided there is mutual love and trust between the generations. But when the basis remains the fear of punishment, the disciplinary commitment is often led by fear and is easily transformed into either opportunism or defiant nihilism.

Without an inner philosophy people cannot be consistently committed. The coercion with an ideology can force people into passive commitment and accepting responsibility in a submissive way, but the inner confusion remains and can burst out in rebellion.

Psychological responsibility. Nobody is completely aware of the 'nature and quality of his act;' usually we only know our surface motivations. Again, a man can do the right thing for the wrong reason, and the wrong thing for the right reason. Subtle inner contrasts determine what course of action will be followed. I might cite the case of some socially well-to-do parents who urged their unmarried daughter to give up her baby for adoption. From the outside it was as if nothing had happened. No stigma was attached to the girl because nobody knew; no legal transgression was involved. But the girl had transcended an eternal biopsychological responsibility about the mother-child relation and was not able to overcome her deeply repressed feeling of guilt. She got married and had children, but her guilt remained, combined with self-punishment, and it took years of psychotherapy and undoing of her guilt to help her become a real, loving mother.

Temporary loss of control is universal. Some people get caught for the misdemeanor; others do not. Psychologically speaking, we may call a person responsible and liable and mature when he is consistent in his actions and when he is able to differentiate between lower and higher values, and can choose and act accordingly. The emphasis is on self-discipline and the ability to put commitment and responsibility first of all on ourselves.

This does not mean that psychology is now able to give a report about the final *trustworthiness* of a person. There exist such strange enclosures in the human mind, representing vengeful irresponsibilities, that we never can definitely say whether sometime in the future they will or will not be provoked or triggered off. Much depends, too, on what opportunity life offers to the person to remain straight. The most tragic moral slips can happen in old age when, on the basis of subtle organic disturbances, self-control can be temporarily lacking.

But we can say that the more a person is aware of hidden unconscious drives and has worked them through with an expert, the more he is able to check them. We can also say that the more consistent training there is in disciplinary self-control, the less chance there will be for irresponsible outbursts.

NORMALITY AND ABNORMALITY

Without investigating the problem of norm and value it is impossible to get a straight insight into the concept of responsibility. The word normal is derived from the Latin *norma*, a carpenter's square, a pattern, the usual rule, the sense of standard. The word is most often used as depicting an ideal fitting in certain social standards. While eccentric people, usually full of resentment, may look down at normality, other people use the words, normal and abnormal, only in the sense of good and bad. Psychology prefers the term *emotionally healthy*, in which a healthy equilibrium is expressed between inside and outside emotional forces, with the person having enough tolerance and vitality to withstand an attack on his equilibrium.

We can distinguish the following suggestions and thoughts that intrude into the concept of normality:

1. *Normality of function* or *genetic normality*. The function of the mind-body unit is continually liable to change. Somewhere in the depth of everyone some pathology is hidden. Death continually intrudes into life and there are always anabolic and katabolic processes active at the same time.

In our evaluation of normality, a genetic postulate unwittingly

creeps in. Regression towards infantile functioning can repeatedly take over, often depending on how great are the dangers
and stresses to be reacted to. Some cultures accept voluntary and
ritualistic regressions as normal, others as abnormal. A person
sitting in cataleptic ecstatic meditation on Fifth Avenue would
be treated as abnormal in New York, but adored in an Indian
village. Important for our thinking, however, is the fact that the
dominance of infantile defenses and adaptation-mechanisms
– such as, for instance, apathy or denial – are looked at as immature and abnormal.

Statistical normality. Our statistically-minded mechanical age too
often puts the stamp of normality on average occurrences, as if
frequency were identical with normality. Even our scientific
research and our opinion polls talk in averages and mean de-
nominators. This has led to the idolizing of the average conforming man who is easy-going and whose manner is casual while
swallowing up his irritations. He doesn't mind being bored by
life. This average normal man is well adapted and feels himself
well adjusted. But don't ask, 'Adjusted to what?' He is often
permeated with the compulsion to be happy and to conform. He
is able to participate satisfactorily in other people's lives; he can
even play the game of escapism and ostrichism with the others.
He learns to fit the picture other people wish to have of him and
competes with others for social approval and status. He is
appreciated and wants to be appreciated even when it is for the
wrong reason. He gradually learns to forget that in human
culture everybody has to repress drives and wishes in order to
become that 'average well-adjusted person,' normal beyond suspicion.

Intellectual normality. The most advertised standard, the intelli-
gence-quotient, presupposes a common potentiality in man to
grasp the world and its mysteries in a rational way. The emphasis is on fact-gathering, exam-proneness, overt competence and
measurable intelligent strivings. The intellect gets overcharged
as a substitute for emotional growth. Parents have been made
jittery when their children don't reach beyond a certain average
in mass I. Q. tests. Normality has become for them a range-

order on the Binet Scale, and a substitute for commitment to an overall excellence.

Normality and the hallowing of precedence. In the back of the legal mind, the concept of normality is also related to legal habit formation. What was written in the books before determines what shall be accepted as normal now. This thought goes parallel to the way we all conceive reality. From our infantile magic experience we only gradually grow into the *adequatio cum re*. Only when we do realize that we see and hear with prejudiced, preconditioned senses are we gradually able to correct our earlier postulates. Yet, in legal decisions, ancient trials serve as precedents. What was normal for our ancestors is supposed to be normal and just for us.

Man's values are continually derived from human traditions. Traditions comprise our value systems. Yet, at the same time, they block our system of values about what to do now.

Normative normality asks for the fulfillment of personal or group or cultural values. It presupposes a historical, religious, social and anthropological awareness. It follows an inner goal and design, depending on people's more or less conscious postulates about the purpose of life and the ideals they want to realize. Here too is included a search for perfection but this time in the service of greater responsibility. Normative normal people look for values and a goal to live for. The normal man learns to tolerate shock and displeasure, frustration and inhibitions. His capacity for normality is expressed in tolerance capacity and defense capacity. Patience is part of his make-up because he can postpone fulfillment to the future.

It is not the action as such that determines normality but the motivation for the action. Eating is normal, but compulsive eating – to soothe inner woes – is abnormal.

The well-integrated, valuable personality is not always well-adapted but has inner strength to realize where temporary adjustment is in conflict with realization of goals. Much of his strength will depend on the emotional and material investment in him by parents and society. Sometimes he has to withstand their need for perfectionism to become a free, self-reliant person.

He also has to learn to protect himself against the continual contamination with feelings of dissatisfaction imposed by modern Western culture.

Spinoza's *amor fati* is his device, knowing, however, that on different psychic levels the acceptance of fate has different motivational meaning. What can be apathy, passivity and self-pity on the infantile level can be wisdom, tolerance and equanimity on the mature level.

RESPONSIBILITY AND NORMALITY

Let us bring these various operational approaches together by asking ourselves: Under what criteria may we speak of a normal responsible person? This chapter on criteria gives examples only of the multiplicity of the approaches we must use; better and more profound criteria can be found but the emphasis is on the combination to be used.

A man can be called responsible and normal:

- When he is not easily liable to regression;
- When frustrations can be tolerated;
- When a self-piloting ego is in charge;
- When one can consistently depend on him;
- When inner ambivalences are checked and conquered;
- When there is awareness of his limitations;
- When there is an alert adaptability and adjustment to emergencies;
- When he is able to take a stand on the basis of conviction;
- When he is able to sacrifice personal satisfaction to higher aims;
- When injustice can be tolerated in order that it may be gradually corrected;
- When, in the face of opposition, a sense of personal value can be upheld;
- When he is aware of his own sensitivities, biases and vulnerable spots;
- When he can tolerate the facts that his illusions are punctured and is able to correct optimism used as ostrichism;

- When he can keep himself alert in curiosity and amusement, and maintain a zest for living;
- When he sticks to the Golden Rule that in all great religions emphasizes the mutual contract of tolerating one another for better and for worse; that is to say, where there is concern for man's fellow man and the fate of the world.

SUMMARY

The words *responsibility* and *normality*, so intricately intertwined, express various values unwittingly referred to when professionals are using these terms.

In using a psycholinguistic approach, an attempt is made to investigate both the psychodynamic and the semantic implications of the concepts. Responsibility, imputability, amenability, culpability and liability are interrelated connotations with subtle differences in meaning. The heuristic legal question, whether somebody is all or not *compos mentis*, normal or abnormal, complicates the values and judgments to be distinguished. The concept of responsibility can be divided into responsibility for action, a delusion of responsibility, a precocious responsibility, the responsibility for omisson, for thinking, for feeling, and for communication, and the responsibility for unconscious strivings. Many of these divisions overlap each other. Finally the concepts of legal responsibility and paradoxical responsibility are looked at especially in relation to man's moral commitments and the various doubts and ambivalences he has to go through before he reaches the strength of a consistent, trustworthy human being.

In the same way can the concept of normality be investigated. There exists a normality of function, a genetic normality, a statistical normality, an intellectual normality and a normative normality, all referring to different value systems which have to be taken into account as soon as the law requires the expert to judge an abnormal and/or criminally acting human being as to the normality of his actions.

On different psychic levels responsibility and normality have different meanings. The final aim of this psycholinguistic approach is to acquire greater clarification about what we mean when we call a man a strong, responsible, trustworthy and normal being.

BIBLIOGRAPHY

I owe thanks to The Institute of Religious and Social Studies in New York, at whose seminars I gathered much thought and inspiration for this subject.

BRÉAL, M., Essai de sémantique. Paris: Alcan, 1897.

BRANHAM, V.C., and KUTASH, S.B., Encyclopedia of Criminology. New York: Philosophical Library, 1949.

Confidentiality and Privileged Communication in the Practice of Psychiatry. Group for the Advancement of Psychiatry, Report No. 45, June, 1960.

DE HAAN, J.I., Juridical Semantics (in Dutch). Amsterdam: W. Versluis, 1916.

EPSTEIN, E.B., Concepts of Normality or Evaluation of Emotional Health. Behavioral Science, Vol. III, 1958.

MEERLOO, J.A.M., Justice as a Psychological Problem. Arch of Crimminal Psychodynamics, Winter, 1959.

MILLIS, J.S., Responsibility in a Troubled World. J.A.M.A. Vol. 174, Sep . 3, 1960.

NICE, R.W., Crime and Insanity. New York: Philosophical Library, 1958.

PLAMENATZ, J.P., Responsibility. Lecture for the Institute for Religious and Social Studies, New York, March 7, 1960.

PRICE, D.K., Irresponsibility as an Article of Faith. Lecture, Sixteenth Conference on Science, Philosophy and Religion, 1960.

REDLICH, F.C., The Concept of Normality. Am. J. Psychotherapy, Vol. VI, 1952.

REIK, T., The Compulsion to Confess. New York: Farrar, Straus and Cudahy, 1959.

The Role of the Concept of Sin in Psychotherapy. Journal of Counseling Psychology, Vol. 7, 1960.

SMITH, J.E., Responsibility, Scholarship and Interpretation. Lecture for the Institute for Religious and Social Studies, New York, Dec. 19, 1960.

WINDELBAND, W., Ueber Norm und Normalität. In Praeludien Tuebingen, J.C.P.Mohr, 1919.

8. Symbol Appeal and Mental Contagion

What is meant by saying that man is a creative symbolizing animal? The Greek word *symballein* means 'to put together' – thus, in a symbol different functions and identities are thrown together. The result is that a reduction takes place of the pluriformity of the universe. I use the words symbol identity and symbol function in orders to illustrate the different dynamic impact of the symbol. Symbols force us to recognize something but also to do something. In the symbols a condensation of functions and identities occurs.

Human interaction takes place with innate biological signs and with manifold symbolic representations which are typical products of human culture.

In every investigation of human interaction and mental contagion we have to give attention to the fact that the encounter of symbolic behavior in one person – e.g., military salute – and the mere perception of outside symbols – e.g., seeing the national flag or hearing the national hymn – can have a provocative action on the emotions of the observing person. A direct co-movement of something internal with something outside takes place, an arousal of common rapport, an e-motion in the old sense of the word: people are moved by 'Something in Common.' There are many symbols people feel and express in common and symbols have an unobtrusive influence on them. In pathology this co-motion can go so far that specific trigger words can provoke epileptic seizures in preconditioned people. They are moved by symbols rather than by realities.

Yet symbols change in their meaning like words change in meaning. The swastika that in the Orient signified the wheel of eternity became in the days of Hitler the symbol of annihilation, of cruel persecution, of scapegoats and of totalitarian conquest of the world.

Our analysis of the function of symbolization is, alas, impaired by the fact that we have to use symbols, e.g., words, in order to clarify symbols. No experience can be evaluated without the inner transformation from the sensory and nonverbal level to a symbolic and categorical interpretation on the verbal level. The very word we speak translates the primary impression into a meaningful 'gestalt,' learned and inherited from former generations, that is continually molding our thoughts. It all begins with man being a peculiar ambivalent animal who not only lives instinctively his own life but takes also distance from it and looks at his own life. Man is a communicating animal who re-creates the biological signals of pleasure and distress into persistent tokens through which he either expresses himself as an independent entity or hides his inner bearings. Man's highest expressive deed, the word, has become a polyphonous sign, an ambassador of his instinctual archaic needs. Through speech and words man learns to handle symbols; he *condenses* reality into simple verbal signs. The macrocosmos reflects itself in the microcosmos. The very word itself is often symbolized as God's fertilization of the human mind through the ear.

In her essay: 'Psycho-physical problems revealed in language; An examination of metaphor,' Ella Freeman Sharpe[1] describes how emotions which originally accompanied bodily discharge gradually find substitute channels in metaphoric verbal expressions. The spontaneous metaphor used by some patients as a transition to the function of symbolization – e.g., by saying 'I could not stomach him' – proved to be an epitome of a forgotten psychophysical experience revealed by a present-day psychical condition. Especially the sounds of words – e.g., the hissing, biting sounds – betray repressed unconscious infantile experience, reminiscences of the early psychic incorporation of the outside world. In pathology the inability to differentiate between symbolization and reality verification plays an important role. Many schizophrenics fail, for instance, in the ability to recognize the symbol as something divided from the mere sensory impression.

Tentatively we may formulate symbolization as an externalization of an instinctual drive in a condensed form, a substitute and short-circuit conception in order to take distance from the instinctual need. Man lives his life and takes distance from his life. Anxiety and suspicion about the real world must have led to this reduction into a simpler symbolic world. A hint of this symbolic displacement of function is already evident among playing animals. When my dog has had enough to eat, he plays joyfully with his substitute rubber bone, a metaphoric symbol of the real bone. He will not do this when he is hungry. In his play my dog changes; it is as though he temporarily frees himself from his doggish drives.

Yet, symbolization is a typical human way of experiencing and relating to the outside world. It is the unconscious transmogrification of the world. It is the rediscovery outside of what is inside the body. We do not see things as they really are but first as an ur-symbol imprinted by our primary outlook on the world. Whiteness and softness are mother's breast, the eye the window of the world, a giant pole is father, the spoon a feeding hand. But at the same time symbolization means taking distance through the process of identification with the outside image. I and non-I begin to separate. This human function of taking distance and of objectivation later on is always combined with anxiety underneath, which is most probably related to threatening primary body images: the overwhelming breast, the threatening nipple or penis, the poisonous excrements. The primary infantile experiences – the native soil for all later experience and verification – are so different from mature sophisticated perceptions. The recreation of an external condensed world of symbolic token – this self-alienation – frees man of the anxiety of the primary danger of being merely a prey of incoming impulses.

Yet, every symbol that appeals to us brings the eerie past back. The primary instinctual experiences may lead to feelings of gratification or distaste, feelings of belonging or loneliness or self-pity. In every symbol these early experiences are transferred in a condensed way. Yet this is also the reason why the outside symbol forces man unwittingly to regress to the initial repressed conflictuous period that urged man to symbolize and to culturally deprive himself of direct gratification. *This inadvertent regression implied in every encounter with symbols causes symbols to have a contagious emotional action.*

Every symbol, no matter how artificially it may have been constructed, must somehow appeal to man's archaic magic thinking. That is the reason why some psychotics who suffered disturbances during the time of development of their magic thinking do not recognize the symbol as symbol but take it for real in the same way as they make no difference between dream and reality. I remember a 22-year-old intelligent girl who made during her first interview a completely normal impression except when she mentioned several times the name of the firm where she worked as 'Johnson Brothers, *Inc.*' emphasizing the Inc. That word Inc. she had not recognized as a common symbol. Later she proved to be suffering of hebephrenia.

Every magic thought as represented by myths and symbols has a deep appeal to man's archaic mode of behavior. They are often representations of infantile anxieties and collective fears, cultivated by cults and canonizations. The witch, the goddess, the enemy, the eternal scapegoat, the devil and the Messiah are all very much alive in us. Man, normal man, transfers basic needs toward symbolic objects. The man who continually sucks a pipe or a cigar hides his early sucking drive behind the smoking symbol. Many other symbolic actions help us to liberate ourselves from conflictuous instinctual urges, especially if these urges cannot be directly satisfied. Many symbolic actions find also expression in gesture language – the eyes, the nose, the lips, the hands, they all make meaningful gestures. We may say that such a symbolic gesture again evokes a direct unconscious response in the fellow being. Symbols can arouse automatic reflexes of hate and hostility. It is this transformation of an original drive into a flippant token that leads to a multitude of ambiguous feelings. In our symbolic gestural interaction we communicate submission, compliance, rebellion, love and hate, and so on. Gestural symbols often provoke direct counteraction; they may be either sexual or political. Let us not forget that the mind-body canonizes very early its danger signals into symbolic tokens. We all can read directly the frozen fright of the phobic neurosis.

Acts and wishes that are regarded by people as immoral are usually disguised in symbols, for peole are afraid of their direct manifestation. The archaic cannibal in all of us transfers his repressed murderous impulses towards the pugnacious habits of the collectivity. The state is allowed to be an agressive war symbol. Father state – the monolithic deity – may attack and make war with an impunity that the individual conscience does not allow in interpersonal relations. Every name, every catch word, every signal, every flag may have such meaning to satisfy man's symbolic and metaphoric needs. Historic symbols and monuments serve, for instance, as a denial of death and a denial of the continual change in history. Yet, the symbol has a specific cultural meaning because it preserves ur-images of the race and ur-images of the individual by attaching them to later images. It covers up man's irrationality by a condensed token.

SYMBOLS: THE GENES OF HISTORY

The symbol as a historical communication is the inherited psychological gene and messenger of old traditional concepts. Symbols are just as much alive as biological genes are and sudden mutations in symbols can also be observed. Symbols carry the memories of the race. Symbols represent that which is transferred from one generation to the other. Symbols are condensed accumulations of memories, charged tracers in the buildup of our personalities. But this also means that obsolete thoughts and attitudes can survive in symbols and prejudices. The wordsymbols will always contain remnants of that old infantile pleasure of the suckling baby who mouths the breast and then later mouths words and abstractions and formulae with the same infantile bliss – or deprivation. But in the baby, words may also become substitutes for denied pleasures.

THE EMPATHIC IMPACT OF CREATIVE SYMBOLS

There is a relation between the function of symbolization through words and the typical human art of making tools as a lengthening piece of the body. Gesture and sound became communicative tools, technical aids to bridge the space between human beings. The economy involved in the condensation of feelings, thoughts and complicated relationships into words made the structuration of our mind possible. The active child that begins to collect things builds up his own symbol world consisting of words and things. The word is a mnemotechnical silo to the individual, always willing to serve through remembering actions and relationships. In the same way the symbol is the mnemotechnical tracer of the race. Before archaic man was able to express himself in verbal and semantic form, he already painted his magic symbols of art on the rocks of the caves, or condensed his feelings and thoughts in the great buildings and monuments of the past.

Worringer, the art historian, tells us how creatively shaped abstraction forces us into empathy[2]. Every esthetic system acts as a 'pars pro toto' symbolizing a greater thought. The creative enjoyment of the artist provokes in the onlooker hidden creative self-enjoyments. The artistic volition of the one provokes direct empathy or conflictuous antipathy in the other. Something of the representation in the symbolic piece of art provokes the reactivation of long-hidden inner representations. That may for instance be the agonizing quality of the cube, □, the proud impact of the pyramid, △, the warm sympathy aroused by the roundness of the stupa, ⌒, or the pleasurable recognition of other body images.

As said before, many a symbol also represents an image imprinted in our minds by unsatisfied or repressed unconscious drives. Thus, being good and ethical can become an empty symbolic act. We can hate and retaliate with symbolic goodness. Indeed, many children are smothered by goodness. Unknowingly, we recognize the promises concealed in symbols, but we also experience symbolization as an enlightening and sublimating process. Deep within him, man has a general understanding of signs, signals and symbols. They resound in him; he quivers and trembles on hearing them – usually without any conscious recognition. This is why words such as *Fatherland, Cowardice, Honor, Treason, Old Glory*, lure the soul of mankind. Symbols are more acceptable than ideas. Symbols are not understood but directly taken over. We react to them without volition, for archaic feelings are triggered off and drag us forth.

Ancient words and symbols with all their ambiguities and varieties in meaning are used in various forms of seductive psychological strategy to muddle the clarity of concepts. Through the ages shamans, priests, magisters and scientific authorities constructed symbols and related dogmas for us to believe in as a defense against change and innovation. Symbolic portions of thoughts are continually imprinted on us through political clichés, or commercial slogans, or even scientific catch words. Private revelations are thus turned into leading philosophies. With the help of symbols mythic delusions of leaders turn into mass delusions of the people because the symbol (e.g., the swastika and the Nazi salute) triggered off unwittingly archaic mass reactions in those whose psychosomatic body unit reacted with the old juvenile fervor.

Especially the archaic symbols of hatred and suspicion stimulate and seduce people in common regression to infantile anticipations. The mythification of old anxieties gives new hope of revenge. The personal hatred gets depersonalized and transferred onto a mass feeling, the person from now on not bearing any individual responsibility. People unwittingly are forced to identify with what is expressed in symbols. Even the use of symbolic expressions in therapy can become a ritual, a rigid condensation of an enigma. This mostly unconscious identification game can go so deeply that the difference between fantasy and reality can get completely lost.

The old werewolf myth tells us how people first had to identify with a wolf in order to be able to act out their destructive and cannibalistic lusts. At the end of the Second World War Hitler started a werewolf movement among the Nazi youths in order to arouse and attain the same ferocious identification. Symbols are supposed to have magic power like our primitive thoughts. Indeed, we may say that during the Hitler years the German conscience was narcotized by symbolisms. The symbolic impact of the Nazi mythology was so great that formerly normal people turned into criminals, into slaughterers of defenseless women and children. First, symbol and myth demonized the victims, then primitive man was let loose.

We are still demonizing ourselves and our opponents!

THE UNIVERSAL SIGN RESPONSE

We must distinguish between a conscious sign response and the unconscious reaction to a token or symbol. The word as symbol – coming to us at a sensitive time – catches us unexpectedly. It arouses old repressed feelings full of reminiscences of early infantile sign behavior. Dreams are brought back to us, old yearnings, old hates, but most of it at an unconscious level. Official symbols are mostly a mixture of both, of conscious sign conditioning (for instance a sergeant shouting 'ten-shun') and unconscious appeal.

Ultimately, however, in the process of maturation and individualization, the influence of symbols grows weaker, the deep unconscious touch fades, the magic of the symbol diminishes. Many symbolic words die of abuse or overwork, or become banal slogans for the listener. Trademarks as symbols for selling of trustworthy products gradually deteriorate.

Human growth and man's broadening reason is directed away

from unconscious archaic appeal. Man has to transmute the direct biological awareness into mental training. Unlike the insect that enters life equipped with a limited and fixed range of reflexive behavior it will also use in maturity, man has to learn and train to remain learning. He has to acquire knowledge of words. He learns to use signs. He becomes conscious of symbols and – to a degree – aware of their deep significance. He goes further; he makes new signs for himself and varies the old ones. He is touched by the primitive feelings behind words and symbols, but he also seeks the particular individual meaning of the word. He wants his word to become a new word and a new concept, related to a newly explored field of experience.

Nevertheless, every symbol confronts man with his own magic thinking and ancient feelings of omnipotence, for he associates with the symbol more dark feelings than he can express in words. There is a limit to the self-expressiveness of man. Those who want to imprint confusion on people work with symbols only. Reason and intelligence have to work with both symbol awareness and with the notion of its limitations. There is no trademark for the progress of reason.

REFERENCES

1. E.F.SHARPE, *Collective Papers on Psycho-Analysis* (London: Hogarth Press, 1950).
2. W.WORRINGER, *Abstraction and Empathy* (New York: International Universities Press, 1953).

9. The Meaning of Crying

A 25-year-old girl in psychotherapy used her beginning sessions
to weep incessantly. This was her initial form of communication:
no words could be exchanged. Yet, outside of therapy she had
never shed tears. She had been a lonely girl all her life. Her
father had died when she was 1-1/2 years old. Her mother had
taken care of this only child by working as a secretary. But for
the patient it had been a restrained, withdrawn relationship,
since the mother was completely steeped in work and had no
other social contacts. Her mother had married a man of different
religion against the wish of her parents. It was as if the mother
had punished herself for going against family taboos by living
in her self-chosen prison all her life.

Two occurrences brought our weeping patient into treatment.
Half a year previously her mother had died after an operation
and a month before her first session a young man from the firm
where she worked as a secretary had approached her for more
intimate contact.

This information I acquired much later when her continual
weeping no longer interfered with her communications. Her
weeping signified all the accumulated frustration, her total lack
of affection, all the crying and weeping she had never been allowed to express because of a stern, forbidding mother who kept
her under constant control. Finally the patient said: 'Before I
can meet a man I have to get rid of all my tears, that is why I
came to you.'

Indeed, a short period of psychotherapy enabled her to get rid of both her justified and her false self-pity. She poured out complaints about continual pressures and about overwhelming guilt feelings regarding her mother. Her misty-eyed aggression betrayed her ambivalent feelings about her complaints. Gradually, however, the self-pitying reaction stopped.

Secretly she had felt that her mother had killed the father with her stern, rigid behavior which had also kept all the aunts and relatives away. The patient had not been able to cry when her mother died; there had only been a feeling of bitter forlornness. This intelligent girl realized that she had started to imitate her mother and to re-enact her mother's pessimistic defiance of the world – until the young man started to woo her. She had always found him sympathetic despite her mother's warning against men.

What she was not aware of was that she came to therapy with an unresolved grief reaction about her mother's death. Because of her long-standing symbiosis with her mother she had not yet been able to dissociate herself from the introjected mother. Our treatment in a nutshell was the working through of this problem. Separation and departure are not immediately experienced as traumatic, but the more painful is that later phase that the author likes to formulate as the inner *departure from departure*.

The moment the patient's repressed self-pity and old masochistic defenses were worked through, all other problems fell into place and she could start a gratifying relationship with the man whom she eventually married.

It is a universal experience that the moment aggrieved people are able to let their tears flow, their inner tension finds relief and they temporarily cry away their difficulties. That is why we say to them: 'Have a good cry!'

In wartime we used to treat some of the soldiers in psychic shock and paralyzed by fear with tear-provoking stimuli: the smell of ammonia, of ether, or even of raw onions brought about this relieving effect. At the same time it was suggested to the victims that they recall their painful experiences; and then suddenly the previously tense, dry-eyed and overly self-controlled patients started to cry and their sense of misery vanished.

Some had shown the clinical picture of a typical fright-catalepsy, with rigid muscles and staring, dead eyes that make such a deep impression on bystanders[5], but this simple form of mental first aid – inducing an outburst of tears and crying – was for many of them a curative catharsis, their short-cut from tension toward relief.

The best first aid for emotional fainting spells and fear-paralysis still is the use of tear-provoking ammonia.

Yet, our repressive civilization usually does not allow adult men to cry relieving tears. Often children are taught self-control too early in life. Many a parent is so distressed by the child's crying that he treats weeping as something particularly bad. Instead of giving the child affection and consolation, such a parent responds with a cold stare of reproach. As a result of this enforced premature self-control, the child whimpers and may develop defensive eye tics to hide his crying. Eye tics usually mean dry crying. The behavior of parents may usually be explained as a defense against hidden traumatic reminiscences, because crying is a very contagious emotional expression.

In our adult civilization we usually laugh at sentimentalities and venture to weep openly only in the dark of a movie theater where we shed tears when we identify with the victims on the screen and thus get rid of some of our self-pity.

To laugh and to cry are acts specifically human[6]. Man is the only creature who sheds tears in grief, though I have observed tears in grieving dogs. Usually at the age of six weeks, tears begin to flow toward the naso-pharynx. According to Sir Alexander Fleming, the discoverer of penicillin, tears contain a strong bactericidal agent, Lysozyme[3], that from the eyes is conducted to the mucosa of the naso-pharynx. This mucosa is our first line of defense against bacterial invasion since our nasal secretions have bacteriolytic action. Even in older people one of the first detectable symptoms in experimental stress is a swelling of the mucosa of the nose resulting from increased tear secretion. What is regarded as a common cold may sometimes be this local alarm-reaction of the mucosa of the naso-pharynx: 60 percent of cases of flu and the common cold occur on blue Monday and signify the easier giving in to stress reactions. When there is a real epidemic the fantasy of having a flu adds to the image of being sick.

In the process of crying we can distinguish between weeping, crying, sobbing, moaning, groaning, whining, whimpering, wailing, bawling and pouting. The formation of tears can be interpreted as a return of a rudimentary archaic protection, the 'veil' of tears being a biologic regression to the amniotic state when the fetus was surrounded by protective fluid[7]. It may be symbolically called a self-immersion into the amniotic waters. Comparative physiology emphasizes the auto-regulatory and regenerative function of protective secretion in order to keep up an inner chemical homeostasis, in which all secretions, especially those of the kidneys, play such an important role. This process made it possible for sea animals to become land animals. Others interpret weeping as an infantile defensive strategy of the organism to eject and externalize painful stimuli. Those various interpretations all say something valid about the diversity of emotional reponses to ancient biologic adaptive reactions[4].

We find, for instance, that this stress reaction returns in older people, not as weeping but as frequent urination. Everybody who ever had to take an examination remembers that he had to go to the bathroom before feeling sufficient relief from the stressful anticipation. During the war the nightly bombing sometimes led to an epidemic of collective enuresis. The child that is not allowed to weep because of social taboo, or the parents' repression, weeps during the night through his kidneys. But this is not the only cause of bedwetting.

Beside the weeping there is the crying and screaming, the calls of distress, the communication of misery in the service of getting help and sympathy[7]. We all understand these distress calls at once, even in yelping animals. Infants, however, can make a blackmailing message out of distress calls: 'If you don't help me at once, I'll burden your eardrums even more than before.'

Crying and tedious pouting belong to the oldest strategies to burden human empathy.

What we call sobbing consists of the concomitant muscular movements of chest, throat, and diaphragm. They are physiologic movements of loss and separation initially conditioned by man's first escape from stress, the movements at birth which are later conditioned by the infantile threat of loss through bowel production. Even man in pain makes the same writhing and wrestling movements as if he had to wrestle himself out of a dark room.

Wailing, whining, pouting, crooning, and groaning belong to the manifold derivatives of crying, often disguising the original act of crying and sobbing because they are already directed toward the effect they have on fellow beings. Every time I hear a crooner singing on the radio, I see his tears of self-pity; he calls it crooning but it means groaning.

What is usually the grief and sorrow people are crying about? Primary psychic pain is the emotional response to the loss of something we depend on. This may be either a valued possession or a beloved person. Usually various psychosomatic symptoms are combined with this stress and separation syndrome[1]. There is a slight shock and feeling of helplessness, a sense of emptiness and angry indignation. The child reacts to weaning with a whining strategy. The psychic wound is often locally felt as an oral deprivation, a painful empty feeling in the pit of the stomach. The younger and less controlled people are, the more they cry.

Acute trauma and stress are usually followed by various adaptive processes and attempts at repair. Crying and screaming in the young child is not only a defensive reflex but also communicates woe in order to repossess the lost love-object. In a later phase of life children and also older people try to deny the loss, they cannot believe what happened, they withdraw in token mourning, or they laugh off what happened. Following the acute loss, to which people are forced to adapt, crying may be delayed. This is what we saw in the patient mentioned above. Delayed mourning usually betrays a complicated ambivalent relationship toward the deceased.

A more complicated psychosomatic pattern may change the acute tension of grief and loss into a more tolerable pattern of fear and anxiety combined with depressive anticipations. The new pessimistic motto is: 'There will never again be any pleasure and gratification; the world is only a valley of tears.' This mechanism of forsaking all gratification in order to feel more secure already leads us into the intricate psychopathology of early masochistic manipulation of the environment. But we have to go back to our real valley of tears.

Even when in all its simplicity we may call crying and weeping an early psychosomatic defense-reaction, man is the strategist of psychic interaction and can use every bodily symptom the way it behooves him. Man can be choked with tears for many inner reasons, but in every crying spell there is somehow a resonance of an old infantile memory re-echoing the state of once having been loved and having lost that love.

Though most people show similar reactions, they usually consider themselves safe in their sentimentality only when they are not seen, for example, in the darkness of the movies. There they weep by proxy about the distress suffered by those on the stage. The more they inwardly grapple with the same problems, the more they let their tears flow about the victim projected on the screen. But remember it is still crying by proxy, although gradually people manage to sublimate their woes into the more refined tears of empathy and sympathy.

Crocodiles don't cry, according to zoologists, but the myth lets them shed tears after they have eaten up their prey; human *crocodile tears* arise from the false pity we have for those we treat badly. We empathize tearfully with our victims to soothe our conscience.

Tears of relief are shed after a sudden cessation of worry. When there is no longer any need to be brave anymore and to suppress tears and people can let themselves go, tears of happiness and ambivalence burst out[2].

I witnessed this paradoxical reaction in the town of Dover,

England, that for four long years was in the line of fire of the German batteries on the Belgian Coast. During those years the people were very courageous. They lived in shelters and kept their fears hidden behind their smiling masks until one day the Allies swept across the Belgian Coast and captured the German heavy guns. The shelling of the British Coast was ended, but now all of a sudden people became tearful. It was like a mass abstention neurosis caused by the cessation of tension. Suddenly they did not have to fight back their fears and their tears. Nearly the whole town of Dover suffered what the British call a *'nervous flop'* because of the lack of self-control over tension.

The same paradoxical reaction may be encountered in many other circumstances. Tears of joy always hide elements of sadness. Man's crying under happy circumstances is used as a magic protection against potential sorrow. The notion of man's limited time one earth interferes with the joy.

There are also the tears of remorse and spite, the tears of defeat, yet they become so easily the tears of deceit. Many youngsters know that with a strategic shedding of tears they can stage a pseudo-remorse and can blackmail other people into undeserved sympathy.

Then there are the tears of ambivalence and doubt when inner motivations clash and joy is temporarily hampered by great feelings of insecurity. 'Why can this happiness not last?' Other people are kind on the surface but have hatred in their hearts; they again shed tears of self-pity. Their tears are often true crocodile tears because inwardly they are celebrating a nearly cannibalistic feast. Blaming the alligators for such hypocrisy is mere projection.

Indeed, there are also the eternal tears of separation, reminding people of birth and death as the two great traumatic separations. We cry because we cannot stick to happiness, meaning we cannot stick to life as the eternal provider of happiness.

Finally there are the tears evoked by beauty, by the ephemeral nature of things. With our tears we say with Goethe: Verweile doch, Du bist so schön!' (Tarry a while, you are so lovely.) These tears foreshadow the great separation all people are preparing for.

The act of crying forces people to make an inner decision. They can shed tears of relief in order to face new stress or can cultivate crying as a psychologic weapon against those who do not want to accept them.

REFERENCES

1. ENGEL, G.L., Is Grief a Disease? *Psychosom. Med.* 23 : 18, 1961.
2. FELDMAN, S.S., Crying at the Happy Ending. *Am. J. Psychoanal.* 4 : 477, 1956.
3. FLEMING, A., Bacteriolytic Substance (Lysozyme) Found in Secretions and Tissues, *Brit. J. Exper. Path.* 3 : 256. 1922.
4. GREENACRE, P., Pathological Weeping. *Psychoanal. Quart.* 14 : 62. 1945.
5. MEERLOO, J.A.M., Human Camouflage and Identification with the Environment. *Psychosom. Med.* 19 : 90. 1957.
6. MONTAGU, A., Natural Selection and Origin and Evolution of Weeping in Man. *Science.* 130 : 1572. 1959.
7. SZASZ, T.S., The Communication of Distress Between Child and Parent. *Brit. J. Med. Psychol.* 32 : 161. 1959.
8. VITANZA, A.A., Toward a Theory of Crying. *psychoanal. Rev.* 47 : 66. 1960.

10. The Problem of Communication and Our Meeting Ritual *

The therapist-patient relationship is the smallest group to study the pitfalls of social communication and interaction. Yet, even when there are only two people in a room talking to each other, unwittingly an army of additional suggestors and listeners is present who have put their imprint on the two in conversation. As our inter-professional communication too influences and penetrates the interaction with our patients, I like to take a very summary and general view on this process of mutual communication thereby comparing it with what is going on in the psychotherapeutic setting. The subject has become especially important since the road to mental health gets more and more characterized as a failure in human contact changing into a free undisturbed intra- and interpersonal communication.

From the outset, I want to emphasize and define that the communication we talk about, here, is the conscious, unconscious and unobtrusive human communion and empathy and not what the engineers call communication – or information theory, when they really mean a different phase of the process namely the theory of mechanical transmission of messages.

The old adage says that for every communication there must be a sender and a receiver. But now we are already caught in a metaphor. Not every receiver is able or willing to listen. Even our radio receivers have to be tuned to the specific wave length

* Lecture given to the American Orthopsychiatric Association, Los Angeles, 1962.

on which the speaker sends out his communication. Moreover, an intricate mechanism of electrical energy providers, transistors, and energy-reformers decides whether the apparatus will work. In a human analogy it may be said that a tuned ear is not always a perceptive ear, and much less an appreciative ear.

Going back to the sender – in this case the author or the speaker – who knows on what wave length he is broadcasting? What gibberish is he talking? A paper, a desk, and a sound-fortifying microphone in a lecture hall do not make the speaker's noises a true communication. From the very moment he is invited to talk about the social aspects of communication he is already caught in a web of confusing anticipations and suggestions. What does a speaker know about the receptivity of his audience, and what about that bigger group we call society? A couple of days after his acceptance to read a paper, he is asked to send in his outline and résumé through which he is unwittingly forced to plan his 'spontaneous' talk, although he would prefer to speak and discuss directly in a two-way exchange. Then a couple of weeks later the technique of our modern meeting ritual requires him to send in his complete paper because the press and the members have to be informed about his 'golden' words. I am afraid that these months of anticipation usually freeze the spontaneity and directness which is the quintessence of any emotional communication and this is the way psychotherapists want to work with human interaction but nearly never do with their colleagues. I only want to say that the very preparation of a speech binds this official communication to personal pre-arranged constructs and prejudices that take something away from the immediate rapport.

The dilemma is how to communicate about communication without losing that intangible impact on the audience that is the mystery of all communication, where mind speaks to mind, independent of the noises that are made, and independent of the distortion and rigidization by our social rituals.

What intangible quality is it that makes some professional meetings so inspiring, sparkling, and fascinating, while others find us less interested and occasionally even bored? Yet, even in science a certain degree of repetitiousness and redundancy is needed to penetrate the harder skulls, though this redundancy can have a sleep-provoking effect. That is why I want to look at my audience as a clinical example of mutual participation and communication and want to use my experiences in therapeutic groups and seminars as a starting point. Some of my clinical experiences I owe to my work in psychological warfare and propaganda techniques during the Second World War.

One of our common fallacies is that the official speech at a meeting or the initial interview of a patient is designated as one of the best forms of communication. True, the speech may arouse mutual rapport, but it may also prevent it. In the Second World War therapists were very much aware that a well directed questionnaire often got much more information out of the soldiers than a biased interview with all its mutual communicative hesitations. There must be people among this audience who get more out of reading or out of the audio-visio means of television than out of this ritual of collective listening. The technique of mass communication at our professional meetings deserves increased interest and study. The talking, dancing skull behind the desk and microphone – as we usually see the speaker – provides a minimum of rapport and communication.

The type of speaker and communicator plays an important role. There are the authoritarian pushers overfilling their audience with rapid verbal bullets with a nearly maternal smothering instinct. There are the true conversationalists, who continually watch the attitudinal interaction with their audience; they expect you to nod and smile repeatedly. The lecture can also become a continual flirtation. There are the talking-downers who play a sarcastic-sadistic game with their audience. Many audiences respond to them correspondingly with a masochistic giggling and squirming. There are the earnest 'scientists' who, with a minimum of contact, bore the hell out of you with statistical information. There are also the perfectionists who do not want to leave anything out of their lecture and thus lose their line of communication and live in a continual dissonance with their audience. They forget that perfectionism and over-insistence are defenses with which more important issues are evaded. Of course, there are many more types, and they all forget that the noise and music they make often communicates more about mood and emotion than the statement of facts they try to transfer. However the function of scientific communication and of meeting ritual is not mere information of new facts or concepts. It also serves a continual fortification of the existing conceptual formulations. In repetition and redundancy, in variation and reiteration, the concepts sink deeper in and become gradually more our own, the same way it happens in psychotherapy.

But this need for redundancy also has its negative side, as this plethora of repeated information leads to too much disturbing noise in scientific meetings and periodicals, lost in gregariousness and lack of crystallized information. Even about chemists it is said that they spend more time in scientific communication than in their laboratories. From this time spent in communication, only 9 % is actually reading the literature.* Most of the literature is not read, most of the lectures are not heard, and much less is perceived. This, again, makes the problem of our mutual scientific communication an urgent problem. The problem of the lost voices is a tragic one; it reminds me of radio stations during the last war, dedicated to psychological warfare, who never received any report about being heard by an audience.

It is a valid viewpoint in psychotherapy to ask ourselves not merely, 'Where did the patient or the group resist?' but also, 'Where – consciously or unconsciously – did we ourselves, as senders, fail?' Our professional meetings and mutual discussions often are examples of how we fail to communicate and obtain rapport with our colleagues and consequently might also fail in similar ways with our patients. Our verbal prejudices must already have an impact on our therapeutic rapport with patients. I have become very much aware, for instance, what my Dutch accent is doing to patients, even when I am practicing in the melting pot of New-Amsterdam.

* Hudson Hoagland, "Communication and Scientific Information". Paper read before the Institute for Religious and Social Studies. January 16, 1961.

Communication, by its very essence, is a chance play with a variety of signs and signals and finally also with words, a game comparable almost to trying to knock down a row of pins in a bowling game. The more communicative throws we make towards a subject, the greater our chance of expressing its very core. In trying to achieve our goal, we can rely on theoretical and intuitive forms of understanding and also on verbal and non-verbal tools. Communication, however, must be a mutual play activity in which the invisible ball is tossed back and forth from speaker to listener and from listener to speaker. Sender and receiver influence each other mutually. I could stand here smiling and telling some quips and nevertheless communicate more than with all my fact-loaded sentences.

Clear, precise language facilitates communication but it is no substitute for the total process. Unwittingly therapists go even further in their communicative expectations because they assume that man in distress can be helped and cured by means of communication and verbal interaction. They assume that human contact conquers loneliness and anxiety, and that healing words transform man. That is why it is so difficult to speak about one specific pattern of contact with patients; the process of interaction changes by the minute. Silence can sometimes be the epitome of communication, and words merely a mask to cover emptiness.

I have often asked myself what sort of professional meeting and discussion I would like best to attend. My first choice would be not a dry discussion panel but a true *symposium* in the ancient Greek sense: a festive dining and drinking together after the tasks of the day are done. There is the play of words and the interaction of listening, and from time to time I can almost hear Socrates or Plato interjecting fragments of their wisdom. I was once a guest at such a symposium in contemporary Greece. We sat outdoors in the shadow of the Acropolis on one of those purple summer nights full of nostalgic fragrances. There was a minimum of lecturing but mutual communication was at a maximum.

What have *we* professionals done with our lecture programs and our systems of scientific intercommunication? It must reflect something of our patient-therapist relation. When I use the word *we* I mean I am guilty, too. Do we really try to communicate? Are we listening? Or are we allowing ourselves to be passively stuffed with too many concepts? Do we try to convert each other, or do we only come together to share conventional behavior? Our competence to select the words, concepts and speakers as being important has greatly diminished because of the overabundance of verbal feeding. I have been at meetings where the speakers, in true oral dominance, shoved their ideas down our throats with great emphasis on clever verbalization. I have been at oversized discussion panels where the competition to be heard was far greater than the readiness to listen. I have also been at meetings where only the wise fathers or the inbred adepts of a particular scientific school were allowed to speak. That is why I am doubly grateful on this occasion that I, a nonmember and outsider, have been invited to try to communicate with you as an audience.

Indeed, many of our scientific meetings have become a strange ritual where the need to absorb wisdom loses out to the need to be seen and heard and, strangely enough, actually to be bored. Indeed, a ritualistic need to be bored plays an important role in our repeated trips to professional lecture rooms. Boredom sends us straight back to archaic feelings of oral deprivation. I have discovered this same yearning for ritualistic boredom in some patients. Long repressed feelings of deprivation, rooted in an ancient hunger for magic wisdom, seek somehow to be gratified. In a paradoxical way, they try to solve this by chiding and boring their audience – in their case the therapist. Yet, man's passive masochistic defenses, once related to a guilty infantile mixture of curiosity and dependency, force some people to remain empty and unenlightened and to accept only the common hypnosis of the meeting ritual. Such people like to be bored and to be regressed collectively toward the phase of archaic infantile frustrations. They expect golden wisdom and return disappointed from every meeting. As professionals, they seldom read and when they do read, they fail to verify the literature; they use the meeting-ritual as a substitute for activity and deeper inner awareness. The same happens with patients in the negative phase of psychotherapy; a sado-masochistic defiance creeps into the therapeutic relationship.

The need for boredom has its own social rituals. There exist religious sects in which members come together on the basis of idolized mutual *mis*understanding. Were the members of such congregation to understand the words of their preacher's clear and simple sermon, the magic awe of his 'divine' origin would disappear.

From time to time professionals use the meeting hypnosis and the ritualistic participation in science as a substitute for clear thinking. For them only the obscure is important. Indeed, coming together in intimate, talkative panels or even in more dignified committees can become a substitute for action. Consciously, we justify that we will meet our friends and colleagues; unconsciously, we search to gratify archaic oral needs. A more primitive instinct of participation, belonging and passively taking in, replaces the need for action and creation.

But I am not pleading for that mixture of awe and boredom.

Numerous motivations bring all of us together at a scientific discussion. I could not even mention them all. Everyone has gone through his own personal struggles for intensified and clear communication and has brought to a meeting his own private frustrations and anticipations: 'How will the speaker handle the subject?'

Rejection or acceptance of a speaker's words and concepts starts long before the meeting itself begins. Every listener decodes the speaker's message in his own private way. People do not listen only to the words and to what the speaker ably verbalizes from his store of experiences and insights. They often listen much more to their own unobtrusive and unconscious perceptions – you may call it intuition – about what the speaker is communicating or neglecting to transmit. We see this in utter clearness in our schizophrenic patients, who nearly never listen but always interpret the hidden intentions behind the speaker's words. And who among us is without this interpretation mania?

Even in a scientific speech there is a latent communication from the speaker himself: his oral pushing, his coercive needs, his shyness, his scientific curiosity, his wish to be acknowledged, his estimation and appreciation of his audience.

The courage to speak is the courage to reveal oneself and thereby to make oneself more vulnerable. It takes a long time before our patients gain that courage to speak without any reluctance or withholding.

Mario Pei, the linguist, has estimated that more than 700,000 various, yet distinct, gestures can be used in human communication. That is many more in number than there are words in the English language. Even in a meeting such as ours the ambiguous non-verbal communication often plays a greater part in the transfer of messages than the formal and rational formulations expressed in our contact-lazy scientific terms. Shaw once called scientific terminology a jargonized conspiracy against lay people. Our behavioristic sciences threaten to be drowned in such abstruse terms.

Students of man everywhere are chasing after fixed formulas, certificates, credits, points, marks and official labels, because they believe that if one is to have professional significance one must set up a certain sophisticated facade backed by diplomas and membership cards. In order to become an accepted adept into 'science', people are prepared to undergo the most impractical courses of training or conditioning, and thus are in danger of losing their intrinsic ability to apply their skills and talents.

I once had to give an expert opinion in court about a problem of communication. A lady had probably written her will under suggestive coercion, while she was mentally incompetent. Testifying in opposition to my view was a learned counter-expert, who had many more impressive labels of expert knowledge and competence than I but who had never seen or treated the type of patient in question; in fact, he had never treated a patient at all. Yet, I was not allowed to reveal that fact to the jury. In fact, my clinical observations got drowned in an ocean of sophistications.

But clinical examples have also their dangerous impact on our meeting ritual. They are usually made so crystal-clear in their dramatic formulation in order to have an emotional impact. I am always amazed how neatly the facts fit the theory and how easily the patient gets cured. Speakers unwittingly construct 'coercive evidence' – if you will permit me to use this term of William James – in order to catch the audience's attention and not the truth. I could construct many snares of clinical evidence with which to capture the attention of an audience.

Despite such snares, however we generally lean toward the views of the *one* inspired speaker we like to listen to – but not for too long, for the attention span of listeners is usually short. Then follows the discussion. In the free debate, everyone is compelled to identify and co-oscillate with the exchange of pros and cons, but also to think for himself, even when he does not get up to speak. The discussants usually force us out of our listening lethargy in order to nod approval or dissent. Some ask questions out of true curiosity, others fire their pet questions to bog the other fellow down. But even the querulous opponent can liven up the meeting. After this mutual activation of rapport, it is most helpful if the speaker or the chairman briefly sums up the total experience in order to close the circle of communication.

It is my conviction that every speaker at a professional meeting has a specific communicative task beyond the pure scientific information he has to give. The speaker is an actor who represents an important role in our communicative exchange. He must arouse in his audience some insight that is still latent, even though the terminology may separate him from his listeners. By his self-revelation, the speaker reveals something in the audience. This 'Aha' arousing function is most important. In the heat of discussion and in the common laughter, he unwittingly clarifies something in each of the participants. Theoretically he may be wrong, semantically he may be ridiculous, but if he serves as a fiery stimulator, he truly communicates to his audience. That is a way in which the private vices of the speaker can benefit the virtues of an audience.

Comparable processes may take place in the therapeutic sessions.

The therapist does not always talk *to* the patient; sometimes his task is merely to voice what the patient must learn to communicate to himself and others. The sophisticated among us may call this method paradigmatic therapy or Rogerian passivity.

Yet, there are strange anxieties surrounding this concept of a common search for truth at a meeting in which we bring out our whole armamentarium of prejudiced communicative tools. The speaker's primordial fear is that his pretensions will be challenged, that the listeners and receivers will become criticizing senders. Only dogs bark freely without caring about counter-barks. Many speakers tend too much to take command of the situation by forcing themselves to be 'original' and by giving new names to old concepts. They blame others to have lack of depth and of non-understanding. How many forms of psychoanalysis are called not 'deep' enough? Yet, such defensive strategy is the risk and ambivalence behind all forms of communication; communication expresses and hides at the same time. We have the choice of sticking our necks out or masking ourselves behind mumbo-jumbo.

Finally, there exists at our meetings that strange compulsion to be 'scientific' and to do research – this overevaluated word. The man who tries to be simple and clear is called either popular or non-scientific. The words *research* and *science* have acquired a magic abstruse meaning. Yet, every psychotherapeutic session is in itself the most intimate research, and full of method. History is the true laboratory of human behavior.

At a meeting of experts, for instance, held during World War II to discuss troop morale, practicing therapists, who had daily clinical experience about the subject, were talked down by 'experimental scientists'. They wanted to obtain a decisive answer to the question via long-term psychological experiments with 200 monkeys. The tentative but more practical advice of the practicing therapists was rejected as 'unscientific'. The historical method and the investigation of unique events seems to be banned out of the realm of science.

The same confusion about what is communicable happens in

'scientific publications'. Usually, only facts and statistics may be presented, not opinions and 'fantasies'. Quote literature and give a lengthy bibliography, use footnotes, prolix and involved abstruse language – and you will be called truly scientific. Yet, only man's creative fantasy makes history. The only originality of many published communications is in the writer's *quotation-mania*, in the way in which findings supplied by others have been re-arranged. There exists in our clinical psychological exchange a tremendous confusion between original creative thinking and *bibliographic plagiarism*.

Adeptomania and *cultism* must be considered two of the greatest dangers of modern psychological and psychiatric communication. They have hampered much mutual exchange. Many members of our noble profession are expected to bear one or other orthodox label. Yet, many of those labels depend on the coincidental school one gets in. Publications of schools different from one's own are usually not read; original opinions are too easily suppressed or committed to oblivion.

Much of the scientific intercommunication went awry in our discussions. If I don't pledge allegiance to the teachings of specific masters, I can be ostracized in special circles. If I use a term the wrong way, I can get 'slaughtered'. We use too many sloganized shibboleths and meaningless passwords in modern psychopathology. This social and professional pressure on our mutual contacts must somehow influence the contact with our patients.

It is our therapeutic task to bring to life again the dead rot of compulsive metaphors and the outmoded words and thoughts which are burdening our patients. Sometimes we bring forth this illumination and re-animation by silent listening, sometimes by dropping the right word at the right time as a spark in the dark.

Who dares to call the therapist a creative healer and a juggler with words? Yet, our task is to teach the patient to speak creatively to himself again. To accomplish this, however, we must drop most of our sophistication and scientific jargon.

Society, with its linguistic habits, forces us to speak in metaphors; we no longer have the direct 'ur-image' of reality. Man's history puts between him and reality the time-condensed symbols of words and speech. Sometimes the creative artist peeps behind the curtain of rusty verbiage. Sometimes a wise philosopher intuitively leads us to his tower of wisdom.

In therapy, we must continually purify and simplify our speech in order to let the patient find his own unencumbered images and exclamations. But we, psychological therapists, use words not only as simple therapeutic tools but also as a ritual fruit and verbal camouflage on many, too many, learned conferences.

To come back to my early oral wishes, I am sure that our ritual fruit will ripen to make our meetings a more truly festive symposium, a feast of mutual communication.

RÉSUMÉ

A speaker trying to contact his audience with whatever he has to say, is already caught in a web of manifold suggestions, rituals, and coercions. His illusion of persuading his listeners clashes with their defenses and their subjective anticipations. Over-preparation of his paper, a cut-and-dried résumé and an extensive bibliography, plus the growing habit of reading papers rather than searching for a direct rapport with an audience through the spoken word, takes away the spontaneity of mutual understanding.

The lack of communicative impact of speakers and listeners caught in their meeting ritual can be analyzed and judged. Examples of such communicative defenses are given.

The analysis of our actual rigorization of communicative exchange is of importance because a similar web of communication is used in the subtle exchanges between therapist and patient.

The study of mental contagion and psychic infection shows even more than the individual analysis of man, how intimately emotions and behavior are tied up with environment and with man's biological and historical past.

The unique individuality gets a better chance to assert itself when critical assessment of existing persuasions and suggestions can be made and when the person is able to distantiate himself from the maze of conscious and inadvertent persuasions that are constantly molding him.

LITERATURE

BERNE, E., 'Concerning the Nature of Communication.' Psychiatr. Quart. April, 1953.
BIERSTEDT, R., 'The Ethics of Communication.' Lecture, The Institute for Social and Religious Studies, New York, February 20, 1961.
LASSWELL, A.D., 'The Ethics of Conference Participation.' Lecture, The Institute for Social and Religious Studies, New York, April 17, 1961.
MEERLOO, J.A.M., *Conversation and Communication.* New York. I. Univ. Press, 1952.
OSTWALD, P.F., 'The Sounds of Human Behavior.' *Logos,* Vol. 3, 1960.
PEI, M., *'The Story of Language.'* Philadelphia, Lippincott, 1949.
STRAUS, E.W., 'The Sigh' *Netherl. Journal for Philosophy,* Vol. 14, 1952.

11. Plagiarism and Identification

The cases of unconscious plagiarism, mentioned in this paper, have clinical interest because they are related to the more intricate problems of unwitting identification and imitation. The growth of our scientific concepts rests on these phenomena. The Latin word *plagiare* means to steal. The root *plak*, in Greek *plekein* means to weave in. Yet, this is what we all do with words. The word plagiarism is related to the English to implicate and to weave into. Milton said: 'To borrow without bettering is plagiarism.'

In the year 1932 a well-known European historian published a book about his own findings in which literally a couple of pages from a book written by a famous colleague were printed as if they belonged to the author's writing, without any mention of the origin of these ideas. A storm of indignation arose after the discovery. The honor of the University got involved and the question was posed if disciplinary measures had to be taken.

The professor himself, who until then had been beyond any blame, was himself very upset and pleaded complete unawareness of his plagiarism. He had worked for years under strain during the gathering of the immense material to be condensed in his book. A committee of experts was chosen to give final opinion to the university authorities. In my own report I emphasized various points that could explain the scientific slip. Under the strain and pressure of work several *mistakes* could have been made by a bonafide scientist without him being consciously aware of it.

The author of the book had a nearly photographic memory which could have led to an involuntary reproduction of what had been read in the other book. This could have been more likely since he agreed and identified with the ideas of his more famous colleague. Hawkes said to Samuel Johnson, 'You have a memory that would convict any other of plagiarism in any court of literature in the world.'

It could also have been that during the year-long gathering of notes and quotations the source of the quotation was unobtrusively omitted and then years later not being recognized anymore as not belonging to one's own work. Although this is a grave mistake and subject to criticism, I could mention that such mistakes were promoted by the increasing need for quotations in the behavioral sciences. The pressure of this ritualistic quotation mania, which had become a synonym for 'scientific' in the behavioral sciences, forced those who published to gather complete bibliographies and elaborate quotations in order to be looked at as completely informed. This need for completeness, replacing the emphasis on clear ideas, increased the chance of error in quotations and diminished the distinction between what is one's own work and what the compilation of other's travails. The fact that he was helped in his huge compilation by several assistants could not exclude that the initial faulty omission was committed by one of them.

Moreover, it could be accepted that the blamed author, who was suffering of high blood pressure and was supposed to have had a slight cerebro-vascular accident, might have shown symptoms of *cryptamnesia* in which the unconscious perceives texts without conscious awareness though it may be reproduced later. In a state of diminished consciousness there may be an increased mnemic potential completely outside conscious perception, we would now call it a subliminal perception. Charcot has described such cases as hysterical cryptamnesia. A maid-servant, treated in his clinic, was able to cite long texts in the Aramaic language which she seemed to have perceived years before when she used to clean the room of her workgiver, a minister who was studying Aramaic while speaking his texts aloud. In psychoanalytic terms we may say that a partial amnesia for the source of the information fragmented another part of the unconscious mnemic storage as autonomous. In neurological terms we can relate it to the syndrome of anasognosia, a lack of awareness of the patient's own functional failure, which often can be related to a specific lesion in the brain.

The author of the book was finally exonerated from any malicious intention or blame.

Since this experience the fact of conscious and unconscious plagiarism remained in my mind, because psychiatry as a partial historical descriptive discipline and for the other part as a natural science, heavily rests on the quotation of authorities. Yet, what is usually overlooked is the fact that the very word we speak is already an act of plagiarism through which we give expression to what through the ages was condensed as meaning into that word. O.W.Holmes said that 'Honest thinkers are always stealing from each other.' The word psyche, for example, the root of the word psychiatry, not only means what our teachers define it to be as a hypothetical subjective side of behavior that can be subdivided according to various actual psychodynamic schemes. In that very word unwittingly many old meanings of the concept reverberate, such as the spirit living in our body, the essence of life, the piloting mind, the animistic soul, the steering inner structure, the totality of unconscious and conscious strivings.

During man's growing up he absorbs and internalizes from his environment and from his history and culture the multiplicity of meanings condensed in his verbal communication. He plagiarizes without knowing it. At best he recreates or reformulates what he assimilates from his own epoch. Originality is a very rare form of creativity. Emerson said of Shakespeare that he was more original than his originals. Yet, the illusion of originality, rooted in our infantile feelings of omnipotence and omniscience, drives many people into a continual search for acknowledgment and appreciation of being a first rate designer of new thoughts. The cliché that somebody has written a 'thought provoking' article or book is usually the best critic one can get in scientific circles in which the critic usually implies that the author may be original but he cannot completely accept his ideas.

In psychotherapeutic practice one sees repeatedly that a patient in the phase of positive transference and complete identification begins to speak 'his master's voice' and unwittingly reproduces his concepts, hobbies and mannerisms.

An intelligent high school girl 16 years old was brought to me by her parents because she developed a depressive state with convulsions shortly after the death of her grandmother. Internal and neurological research was completely negative and gave no explanation. Psychological exploration showed that the girl had had a strange submissive relation to the deceased grandmother. She slept often with her grandmother in the same room. The grandmother brought her to sleep by bringing her under hypnosis. She had learned this method after living for years in the Orient. As a matter of fact, this grand lady had kept the whole family under a kind of hypnotic spell, awe and submission.

The initial diagnosis of the convulsive child was hysterical twilight state, resulting from a sudden loss of her proxy, with whom she had completely identified. The consulvions could be explained as a sudden abstention syndrome after yearlong repeated hypnosis. There was no personal ego to control the primitive impulses suddenly coming up from the unconscious after having been controlled by an alter ego.

Indeed, in the patient's dreams the most ambivalent feelings toward the deceased were expressed. There was the need to murder her and to break the chain of dependence, but also the need to jump in her grave and to join the dead. At one period of the treatment the call of the deceased became so great that a short-lasting hospitalization was needed to prevent suicide in a twilight state.

The character of the convulsions was of a classic epileptic state with complete loss of consciousness, loss of urine control, retrograde amnesia and a post convulsion twilight state. The convulsions disappeared in one month after the onset of psy chotherapy without medication.

In the course of two years of psychotherapy with diminished frequency of sessions the provoking memories of the grandmother got more and more repressed and the girl developed in her school as a more brilliant student than before.

A new problem came to the fore: the complete identification with the therapist. Hobbies were taken over and the therapist's professional aims. The analysis of this transference took great pains to explain – although said in more popular terms – how the ambivalent identification with the deceased grandmother was transferred towards the therapist. All this was worked through in good grace with the emphasis on repressing the past and under the condition that if she really wanted to become a physician she would go back in analysis during her residency. As the girl came from a family of physicians I could in her professional aim not completely allude to the transference.

I saw her the last year infrequently until she came back with the message that she had to leave college because she had committed plagiarism. She pleaded to me that she had not been aware of it but that the professors did not want to believe her. Her task had been to write a critical essay on a book that I had happened to review for one of the newspapers just in the time we had been on the heights of the transference and she had read faithfully my ponderings.

Plagiarism by a student who has to write his own critical opinions is, indeed, a misdemeanor, the faculty has to give attention to continually, otherwise the aim of education to independent thinking would completely get lost. In this case, however, I could explain to the faculty that by coincidence, because of the choice of that special book, unconscious processes had led to the student's unwitting identification with the author of the book review and consequently she was reprieved of the charges.

For reason of simplicity I omit in this clinical survey the intricate question of primary and secondary identification and the ambivalent tendencies behind this creeping into somebody else's skin. Yet, it has important implications for the student of psychiatry since the various theoretical schools and psycho-dynamic schisms often overemphasize the process of identification with the students' teachers and masters. Adeptomania is the risk of all teaching.

Also, an opposite form of negative identification and omission of quotations can take place when the author happens to belong to a 'hostile' school. I remember a lecture where a member of a rivaling school was invited as a discussant and where his work was quoted with great praise. Yet, when the lecture was published his contributions were omitted. Another negative form of plagiarism is the growing tendency to refer only to the last years of scientific literature thereby denying the fact that all human communication and thought is rooted in a long line of historical development.

I want to finish by quoting what the British author, Charles Kingsley, said: 'No earnest thinker is a plagiarist pure and simple. He will never borrow from others that which he has not already, more or less, thought out for himself.' We may now say: this is true in general provided one takes into account the unwitting transferences, identifications and antagonisms that beset all human beings.

RÉSUMÉ

Two cases of unconscious plagiarism are mentioned. The various way unwitting plagiarism can occur is elaborated on. Plagiarism can be an act of conscious deceit but there exists also an unobtrusive plagiarism dependent on the normal processes of communication, learning and human interaction.

12. Reading block and television apathy: An alarm for parents

Reading block of the school child is at this moment the most frequent social neurosis in New York City. Nearly one-third of the grade school population has it.

Usually our medical and psychological diagnoses – such as the reading block of the child – cover up a multitude of human failings but also a multitude of diagnostic sins. Sometimes a few individual clinical cases tell us more about the intricate disturbing family relations than do a pile of sophisticated statistical findings about what can only be considered from a personal, nonstatistical angle.

I am aware that reading block, as part of a communication disturbance, can be caused by a complicated failure of the mind in which congenital dyslexia, retarded mental development, distorted visual function and brain damage play an important role; but usually reading block results from lack of motivation or paradoxical defenses against reading.

In this chapter I want, however, to concentrate on the normal, 'nonstupid' child possessing good intellectual potentials, or the gifted youngster who is thrown into a world of communication habits with which he cannot cope. He may, sometimes, even have a superior intellect, but his perception has been emotionally disturbed because the troubled child has been living in a family circle with which he had confusing or no contact. Often one of the parents may be depressed or withdrawn, or there exists a burden of anxiety provoked by intrafamilial conflicts.

Consequently, such a child has not developed an alert and adroit *communication facility*. In such circumstances, television – the hypnotizing screen in the living room – acts proportionately more disruptively because it will be used with all eagerness as a paradoxical defense against loneliness, yet, gradually promoting a more intensive feeling of loneliness.

In many cases the emotional disruption in the family can be overcome by very simple psychotherapeutic means, thus making unnecessary the whole rigmarole of reading clinics and remedial reading methods. I have also seen children who defiantly declined to read because the class was too slow for them.

At the outset I want to emphasize that this is not an article pro or con television. I am not one who believes that men are so easily changed into neurotics. But television can unwittingly serve to bring the hidden frustrations in the family to the fore. Every form of mass communication can be used for the wrong or the right purpose. Besides this, every technical development has unobtrusive implications for man's physical and mental existence, the right awareness of which can help us to correct them if they bother us. We can no longer escape the age of technique and institutionalism; the greater need is to correct its possible destructive impact. The million-fold multiplication of information sent out daily unwittingly directs itself not only to the intelligent verifier and analyst of news but also to the common denominator of man – the faceless person with the flabby mind, who is easily coerced into believing.

At this writing – the fall of 1961 – reading habits of older persons also are influenced by various technical means and distractions. A man who is dragged by his car along the road cannot read. A child imprisoned in the back seat during the weekends, while the parents bicker about which way to go, cannot read. Adolescents beset by precocious and confusing dating habits do not read. A recent poll brought out that 60 per cent of first-year *college* students had not read a book voluntarily during the past year.

Years ago I described a neurotic reaction calling it 'television apathy,' in which the child shows itself unwilling to have personal relations other than with the spellbinding, fascinating TV screen. Children between four and six years of age were found able to communicate easily with the TV screen but not with their parents. These children form a compulsive, symbiotic relation with the lively screen.

True, the parents started the problem by being fixed to the TV screen themselves, hardly speaking to one another because of that nearly hypnotizing effect of this new toy and celestial eye. The intimate function of reading aloud to the children was not exercised any more. The gadget became the new technical nursemaid. The mother works in a factory or office during the day; at noon the children go alone to the automat to put their dimes in the slot and to receive their food mechanically. Lifeless tools substitute for the paternal function of taking care and 'giving affection.'

Unobtrusively there has crept between children and their parents a mechanical world of gadgets which keep the family members farther and farther apart emotionally. There is never any fun. There is never any reading aloud as a stimulating example and token of family unity. Gradually no real, warm feelings are exchanged any more. There is no longer any time, since everybody has to watch and listen to the electronic substitutes for communication.

In many homes we can detect a fear of the vacuum of silence as if meditation and thinking were ridiculous functions. The quizzes emphasized the accumulation of mere facts without the wisdom of their interrelation. The screen is full of antisocial persuasions, not to mention overt pollution with deceit and crime. Radio and TV have brought into the home an avalanche of redundant noises, interfering with the family as a communicating community. The absorptive and selective capacity of our ears and eyes and minds is continually coerced by outside programs at the cost of interpersonal exchange. There is a constant barrage of pictures glamorizing adult violence, trigger-happy clowns, stealth and sexual excitement, while advertising thrives on increasing the listener's dissatisfaction, thus making us into the richest society with the deepest feelings of dissatisfaction.

Language is a means of self-expression, but in many millions of cases the gadgets have taken over, repressing the creative function of playing with words – 'Be quiet, I want to listen to the radio!'

Reading is an active creative process, translating the printed images into feelings and thoughts. The active, creative game of speaking and reading is easily disturbed by technicalities about how to learn to speak and read. This is also true for the too-rigid technicalities in the schoolroom or reading clinic. The child picks up the function of condensation of thoughts into symbols in continual verbal *exchange* with others only – that is to say, through trial and error, answer and response – not, however, through merely passive listening. When this playful exchange is not provided, a greater dependency on technical sources of verbal exchange begins. This is the time the reading block begins to develop.

No wonder the children refuse to learn to read, spell and write in school. The sophisticated letter image is much less fun than the more easy-to-grasp picture image on the screen, and besides, there are plenty of spoken words coming from radio and TV. Instead of the printed communication, the children secretly crave a warmer, direct verbal communication which is so badly lacking in their homes, where the ancient art of conversation has disappeared. Their reading block becomes a passive act of sabotage. Indeed, various cases of reading block could be attributed to a lack of affectionate parental sounds and parental intercommunication. The reading of words and books, as initiated by the school, is consequently experienced as an act of separation. Many of the reading block kids have school phobia that also signifies separation-anxiety. The children want to cling to an illusion of mother's golden words soothing them into blissful oblivion.

Reading is a highly complex psychosocial function involving various forms of verification of reality. It asks for greater awareness of the process of symbolization, that is to say, of condensation of meaning in a single token. It creates a greater distance from the affectionately spoken word and demands extra activity in learning. Our present emphasis on rapid reading, on reading pacers and faster reading habits is a big hoax and is inclined to make the overapprehensive parents even more smothering to children. The child does not read with his eyes but with his mind, when freed from inhibiting emotions.

What we are apt to call reading block in the child consists, in the majority of cases – according to my experience – of the child's unconscious refusal to progress from the promiscuous, spoken communication representing, to him, private attention and to enter into a lonely dialectic relation with the printed word.

The function of the analyzing reading eye and mind is different from that of the hearing ear. The eye verifies critically and can return to what it has read before for renewed evaluation. The function of focusing can already be emotionally disturbed in a child who has seen too much 'ugliness' in his environment. The ear by its very function has to be more acceptant and even submissive to what it hears because it cannot return to what it heard before.

Our individual mental *freedom and independence start with the written word we can verify*, although the holy writ can become secondarily an omnipotent command. Listening and talking are always a collective interaction; reading, an individual action in a private corner.

Reading block in the gifted – the child's passive defiance of and defense against the parents' addiction to gadgets and automats – makes him, nevertheless, more submissive. *Dependency is always the paradoxical friend of defiance.*

Learning to read is hard work for the child; it requires inner motivation and example of hard work done by the parents. Reading alone in a corner is a symbolic act of independence, taking a token distance from the world. It makes man into an inquisitive, observing personality. Man lives his life and man looks at his life. Reading teaches a child to take observing distance. It teaches empathy with other beings and thus enlarges the self. Later, it can again be used as a form of withdrawal.

When the parents are addicted to the radio or the TV screen, the child interprets this as a lack of love and approval. The parents shush him and want him to be silent. How can the child put forth effort when the daily catch-word is: 'Take it easy'? How can a child be motivated to read if there are no books in the house? The screen at least talks to the child, plays with him and takes him into a world of magic fantasies. For those children the gadget is a substitute for the grown-ups and is even forever patient. The child translates this patience of the gadget inwardly into love; the machine is never as irritated as the parents.

In 1958, 4,000 out of 16,000 seventh graders from the New York City schools could not be promoted because of a reading block. For 25 per cent of the children, the reading ability was at the fourth grade level or lower.* In 1961, 10,000 children, also seventh graders, could not read third-grade books, according to the superintendent of schools, and 50 per cent of the junior high school pupils were more than two years behind in reading.** This points up the size of the problem. A recent publication even speaks of 40 per cent of bad readers.***

In 1958, the City of New York had to stop its policy of automatic promotion in the schools when it was found that some youngsters promoted to high school were unable to read or write. The lack of competitive incentive played a role here too. The cost alone of having the 15,000 non-reading elementary pupils repeat a year of schooling would come to nearly $ 8 million.

Usually the educators try to give these children a rather costly remedial reading therapy in which, with the help of psychological gadgets, the child is reconditioned to reading habits in a patient way. In various cases I found out, however, that the child experienced this psychological therapy as a repeated coercion, arousing all his old resistance and defiance – formerly accumulated toward the parents – toward the reconditioning psychologist. There is also too much of a tendency to attribute reading block to faulty methods of teaching to read – e.g., the 'whole word method' as against the separate 'letter' method – at the cost of giving attention to emotional factors. I have seen the children

* *New York Times*, June 24, 1958, p. 28, col. 6.
** *New York Times*, April 15, 1961, p. 1, col. 2.
*** *New York Times*, October 31, 1961, p. 33, col. 1.

fail with both reading methods. It is the deindividualizing habit of *all* methods that provokes the defiance in the child.

The fact is that fewer mothers teach their youngsters letter-reading and the method-bound teachers resents it when the child can read already. I know of teachers asking the parents not to teach their youngsters before they come to school. The teachers feel coerced in their good rights. They forget that the conditioning to attentive reading starts in the parental home and not at school.

In one such case the boy could read when he entered grade school but was teased so much because of his abilities that he gave it up in a desperate masochistic maneuver.

True, remedial reading exercises are indicated for children with neurological and sensory reading block or those with disturbance in 'Gestalt-apperception,' but where the cause is an emotional trend in the family or the class, the parents have to be alerted and the decaying family structure or the boring teacher has to be treated. Again, therapy is very easy in many such cases.

In various reading problems I could, for instance, urge the father to give more private attention to the child and to play Scrabble – a competitive word game – with the children instead of watching TV. Also, both the parents should be reading more as an example.

We may describe, in short, the psychological task of the father as bringing the child from the more biological and emotional realm of the mother toward the more rational confrontation with social issues. In psychoanalytic jargon, we say that the father is normally the first transference figure in the child's life. The father cuts the cord. Bringing a rather passive father back into the family circle as an active playmate does not directly influence the child, but it indirectly changes the family structure for the good and makes both the parents more aware of their role and example in the communicative exchange inside the family.

In several cases of the combination of school phobia with reading block, the fact that the father took over the mother's nagging attempt to imprint the child with letters and words had its liberating effect on the child. I knew a defiant youngster for whom *not reading* meant not willing to be fed by mother.

In various cases the child overcame his reading block as a result of a changed, warmer attitude and family involvement on the part of the father. The whole family gained in self-reliance and greater cheerfulness by this mental hygienic propaganda for the conversational family circle, under the protection of the participating father.

Mutual relation and communication are needed not only in the service of love but also in the service of man's growing self-esteem and in the formation of a selfpiloting ego. The reading of printed words leads much more to the individual freedom of verification than the dependency on spoken messages. A non-reading youth becomes an immature, dependent youth.

Besides the unobtrusive technical invasion into family intercommunication, other disturbing interference by radio and television exists which is too much poohpoohed by those economically dependent on spreading this form of information.

The pollution of rivers is limited and controlled by law; the pollution of the air arouses everybody's fury, but mental contagion through the ether is allowed to hire its own channels. Civilization has to teach people to protect themselves against what they greedily want too much to consume. The television 'servants of the public' do not do that. Because of their emotional investment in their profession they have to create an atmosphere of adulation, of mass coercion and mass contamination. Under the euphemism of public relations, the magic fantasy of manipulating and engineering public opinion is strongly alive.

The daily dose of televiolence, of excitement, horror, fear, murder stories, criminal sadism and crooning self-pity inhibits the building up of inner moral values that, in the initial phase, belong exclusively to the realm of the family and not to an intruding, hypnotizing screen.

Much depends, of course, on the sensitivity and vulnerability of the hearing minds. The commercials pound their daily suggestion of dissatisfaction into people's heads, combined with the 'jingles of greediness.' The intervention of commercials promotes the dislike of reading. Sensationalism leads to withering social compassion. The empathy with the screen suppresses the sympathy with men. We are gradually becoming a nation of Peeping Toms instead of thinking individuals.

Within the last 10 years I have been asked for advice in several cases of increasing mental apathy leading to a pseudoschizophrenic mental picture. In each case the child refused to leave the television screen. Most of these children were in their early adolescence. They neglected their school work and home duties. They showed a withdrawal from reality, although they were not psychotic. Some gradually became more negativistic, got out of bed only to look at the television screen – especially during free weekends and holidays – and apart from their television interest, showed a general apathy toward everything.

Mary, a girl of 15, was sent from school because she failed in all subjects. The last two years she showed a sabotaging attitude, skipping classes, or sneakily looking at comic books during class hours. At home she showed every sign of television addiction. A psychologist had already made the diagnosis of schizophrenia, based on the increasing symptoms of apathy and lack of mental contact. First, I tended to agree with the diagnosis. But gradually I found that she was more willing to relate to me when we started to talk about the television programs. Then the girl became vivid, showed interest, told about her wishes to take part in the programs, and so forth.

It took several sessions of psychotherapy to make her better aware of the fact that she had completely surrendered to fantasy life. The process of weaning from the screen provoked much resistance, and a rather primitive noncompliant attitude on the part of the parents did not help either.

It was pointed out to her that television gave her, in a cheaper and easier way, what she would otherwise have obtained from unreal fantasies, as defense against an environment she felt as hostile. The deeper causes of her flight from reality were gone into and could be explored. Gradually the girl gave up her 'screen sessions' and her television trance in order to start a new emotional investment in reality situations.

In another case, where an underlying disturbance was directed toward plain flight into fantasy, it was more difficult to lead the patient to give up these pathogenic escape habits. I call them pathogenic because, secondarily, they fortify underlying neurotic tendencies. Eerie, weird, panicky stories disturb the child because of his weak ego. They settle in his fantasy, fortifying other anxieties.

A school survey in a middle-class suburb of Buffalo found* that kindergarten tots are at their TV sets at home 50 per cent of their classroom time. But as the pupils grow up to the sixth grade, they devote nearly equal time to school and TV.

A school official concluded: 'Television is changing American children from irresistible forces into immovable objects.' This stealer of time hypnotizes many people – especially children – into indiscriminate watching. The magic tie with the TV screen promotes a more primitive magic relation with mother and home. Like dope, TV promotes TV addiction, a loss of internal control about the use of the medium.

Older people are often seized with panic and depression, provided they are sensitive enough to understand the cynical attitudes to which our television exposes its public. Not long ago one of our medical journals** related cases of impulsive suicide provoked by such anxiety-provoking behavior, and from my own practice I know of a case where a sadistic TV program acted as a trigger for the suicidal act.

Although there is much talk of mental hygiene, the subject of daily toxic mental contagion has as yet not been put under close scrutiny. People do not want to accept the fact that psychic contamination is an accepted phenomenon and that television can be a full or partial contributor to such moral infection. People have already forgotten the overt panic caused by Orson Welles' broadcast about 'the invasion' from the planet Mars. The police can control dope smugglers, but television brings dope right into the homes.

* 'Opiate of the Pupil,' *Time*, 71 (March 24, 1958), 62.
** 'Suicide After Watching Television,' *Journal of the American Medical Association*, 167 (May 24, 1958), 497.

Our technical age has the tendency to make people more passive and more dependent, combined with an eerie feeling of depersonification – that is to say, of not being a unique individual any more.

All this does not imply that people have to do away with the fruits of technology, but, in realizing better its negative psychologic impact, they can restore normal circumstances and prevent technical gadgets from becoming the relation-spoiling intruders in the family.

We must, for instance, assure parents again and again that *they* are the best educators the child can possibly have. They are this because of their biological ties. No lecture, no book or TV or a foster parent can replace the parental impact on the child. No official educator is willing to adopt the endurance and the tolerance of most parents. Those psychologists who have caused parents to be over-anxious concerning their educational task have not served those parents well; rather, they have introduced a strained, over-intellectualized atmosphere into the family circle. Reading must be a shared game in the family and not a nagging task and compulsion.

In the clinic we so often see insecure parents who, because of their own doubt, keep their children in a continual state of suspense. This makes the children even more confused emotionally because they need consistency of affection under the guidance of discipline. There is too much confusion between freedom and spoiling. The child asks instinctively to be loved but under the guidance of discipline in order to build up straightforward inner rules.

Only later when he is on his own feet will he be able to verify the acquired inner pictures with the ethics the world shows him. The psychic distance from his parents, their inconsistency and doubt impoverish his inner world and ego. As a result he will become an easier prey for influences from outside.

By putting all our little antennae in the same ether we have become a symbiotic mass more vulnerable to mass suggestion and technological hypnosis, with greater chance to be molded into conformity.

Paternal authority is needed for the mental activity involved in the normal suppressive and sublimative processes. The parents have to fight the abuse and addiction to TV in the homes by setting the example of restraint themselves. In the same way they have to set the example and to read themselves in order to make the child eager to read.

Above all, no parent can restrict a child's television habits without restricting his own peeping habits. Sometimes simple advice and re-education of the family will help to overcome the reading block of the child. The child usually conquers the world of symbolized ideas without reading machines or reading clinics. Parental authority and discipline are needed to check antagonism and hostility and to change destructive tendencies into constructive ones. When, however, the family ties break down, the child has to build up his own mental defenses. When he is left to himself – in the confusion regarding which morals to select – he often becomes aggressive and delinquent. It is as simple as that. No child will be a nonreader if the Bible is read every morning at the breakfast table. Yet I have seen many families where the communion and conversation around the dining table had almost ceased to exist.

Last but not least, the existence of a reading block in an otherwise intelligent child reports to us that something very basic went wrong in the system of intercommunication in the family circle or the teacher-student relation, a distortion that can usually be repaired if the therapist or counselor gives more attention to the family pattern than to the letter-stumbling child.

13. A World of Smells

In days long since gone by the streets never seemed to come to an end. Somewhere they went on and on for an indefinite distance, ending in a dreamy eternity that was filled with alluring fragrances.

Even now, having returned to my home town, the Hague in Holland, for a brief visit, I feel amazed that the familiar streets are as I remember them. But the old elusive feeling of infinity is gone. It comes to me that I am still looking for a special old tree or a fountain, for a landmark where the miracle of something far away first began.

And then, around the corner, a forgotten magic greets my nostrils – the old familiar sea breeze, the wind blowing in from the ocean and filled with salty delights. From that direction once came the stormwind we used to battle in late autumn, while making our way through the dunes and struggling against the driving rain.

As I walk along I pass my old school and another potpourri of smell memories washes over me ... the scent of wooden floors intermingled with bathroom odors and children's moist clothes that seems to cling to all schools everywhere.

Further on I find again the little harbor with the pungent aromas of various mercantile products – coffee, cheese, and musty wheat flour, as well as the decaying flotsam floating in the water. Here in the park the flower buds open into blossoms after the rain and waft abroad their subtlest perfumes. There down a narrow street lives a wine merchant and always when passing I would try to sniff my fill of the intoxicating odors from his shop. The same thing happened when the baker brought his fresh bread out of the oven. It set my salivary juices flowing in great anticipation.

There I see the old fish market where women in quaint colorful garb sell their husband's gleaming catches. There is no end to the glorious variety of smells. I breathe deeply and with the air I inhale the whole world.

Often, when traveling through foreign lands, I have experienced this feeling of inhaling eternity. When a ship was taking me to some fertile forest-strewn coast, the peculiar scent of that green spot was in the air, like the shadow of Cyranno' nose, long before the vessel reached the shore. It never failed me – that welcoming cloud of smells, of tropical flowers and mouldering decay. It penetrated the salty sea air, giving sweet promise of the exotic experiences that awaited me in the jungle.

Now I head for the old flower market in the Hague with the sounds of the carillon ringing out an obligato for the feast of the senses. There under the acacias the man with the fruitstand always stood, and a little further on was 'the *Waag*,' the scales where the squirming pigs used to be weighed. Walking still further along there would come to me the smell of books, that dark smell that filled me with yearning as it invited one and all to read and dream and collect books.

Alas, the market is no longer there. Practical considerations forced the city council to do away with the ancient feast of smells and colors. I pass the little mews where the horses were once shod, the hoof burned before the shoe would fit, while the onlooker felt the thrill of riding far away over the distant plains. I walk through my home town. Yes, the smells have changed. The automobile with its exhaust has blotted out the delicate fragrances. Arriving at the ruins of the home where I lived before and during the war, I find there still lingers the smell of burning rubble and ashes. Strange that it should persist, so many years later.

Even the odors of the railway station are altered. Now the

trains are electric. Time was when the engines belched forth mountains of steam and covered the cars in a sweet smelling shroud of smoke. When the locomotive started to pant and lurch forward it seemed as if an aroma from the distant horizon enveloped all those who bade goodbye to the travelers. Hot steam still has that magical effect on me – it stirs up my longing to travel.

There is a good explanation for all my olfactory nostalgia. After all, smell is related to our first loving contacts in the world. The newborn infant lives first in a world of pure smells, although the world soon teaches him to forego his notril pleasures. For him mother is love at first smell. When he is older, he cannot sniff and smell keenly anymore because smelling has become taboo. Thanks to the enforced toilet taboos our innate perception of smell degenerates into chemical irritations by soaps and antiseptics. While sexual odors are taboo, man borrows these odors from flowers and plants. The sexual organs of plant and animal – musk, civet and the rose – bring him what he has suppressed in his own life. Nevertheless, something of the instinctual passion for smells remains in man. It cannot be totally suppressed by the most pristine sanitary habits or by chlorophyl-minded merchants. Modern culture has made people feel ashamed of body odor. Whole industries thrive on that artificially induced self-consciousness. They create diseases such as halitosis just to make people feel inferior. Many a girl has become neurotic because she has completely suppressed the role and delights of perspiration.

Be that as it may, smell communication still exists. Every mood and emotion stimulates the organism to produce different hormones and different skin products, the smell of which is subliminally perceived by our fellows. I myself remain ultra-sensitive to smells. Every being communicates to me a different odor, whether pleasant or unpleasant, attractive or repelling. I often dream of familiar smells, of my father's pipe, of being back in the kitchen of my childhood, of pine woods in the rain. The odor of girls I have loved still takes me back in dreamy ecstasy to the days of my youth.

Clinical medcine has known for a long time that diseases have their special odor. I am convinced that different personalities can be differentiated by their smells. Curiously, it is not my nose that warns me that the smell of the room or the person is bad. What happens is that I respond with a body reaction, with a headache – a defensive tension against any smell perceptions. My brain grows dull and I have to get away from the situation.

Friends have often asked me to tell them what my favorite smell experience is. Whereupon I always sing my paean of praise for the olfactory ecstasy of climbing mountains. All day long the sun burns down upon the trees. Gradually, as you work your way up, those woody smells give way to the grassy ones of the Alpine meadows, until you reach the higher regions where there is only stone and snow. You reach the top of the mountain and the high winds play upon your nostrils.

At that moment for the first time I feel free – free on top of the world, free from the compulsion to smell all those people below, each one wrapped in his own soulless deodorized mist.

14. To Honk or not to Honk!

THAT PARADOXICAL NOTION OF NOISES

One morning in New York I awoke unusually early. I found myself tossing around and turning my body axis again and again, sensing that something strange was fermenting both in my dream world and outside it. There it was: the great paradox of silent emptiness. The city was strangely quiet as if suspended in dead empty space – no rattling of cars, no throbbing or rumbling of motors nor honking of horns. Full of apprehension, I was waiting until in the vague distance I heard it slowly coming: a truck. A heavy gasping and coughing truck came arrogantly sawing its way through the silence. The traffic light on the corner of my street must have turned red just then, because suddenly the truck's sputtering motor stopped, only panting like a prehistoric beast, waiting for its prey. – Then suddenly, the whirring, rickety motor started up once more with a scrunching sound as if someone had awkwardly dropped sand into the engine. The truck continued on its way. Its gasping, dying cadenza provided a welcome relief for my ears. I turned over with a deep sigh and fell quietly asleep again.

The day I heard that honking and tooting had become a punishable act, I appreciated very much the concern of the wise and noble city fathers of our metropolis, and their wish that my rest and relaxation should be undisturbed. From now on every shriek of autohorns breaking upon the quiet air was to alert the corner policemean with his ticket book. No longer was any driver to be allowed to disturb the peace of the metropolitan air by honking fretfully at innocent pedestrians and competing drivers. People had already tolerated the rumbling, growling and honking cars too long – and their numbers were ever increasing.

Yet had the citizens really felt tolerant of all those two hundred horse-powered vehicles? Not only their noise but their expanding size threatened to choke the narrow limits of the isle of Manhattan. Metropolitan space and parking space have become synonymous, and there no longer exists the quiet meditative atmosphere of strollers which was so familiar to our forebears. Indeed something drastic had to be done.

The noble fathers of the city are quite right to declare war on the noisy motorized invasion into our peace of mind. Noise is noise and to honk is to honk. After the persistent rattling and honking has done its part in making the modern citizen neurotic, who is to provide for him a soothing balm so that he may relax again?

Yet that sleepless silent night made me ponder the difficult science of noise – noisology let us call it since no term exists to describe it. I was sure, paradoxically, on that night in which I tossed and thrashed about, that it was for lack of the frivolous honking and hooting on our avenue that I had been kept awake. Noise belongs to our technical age like butter to our bread. Your sensitive author lives in the very center of New York and is so conditioned to his nightly noisy lullaby from the street that the quiet and silence kept him tossing and turning.

By the way, I had never myself realized before that our city was actually flooded with the disharmony of screaming claxons. It was only now and then that I could hear a superfluous screaming toot as for instance caused by the honking-call of sweethearts to attract some late evening dates. But who would dare to interfere with so intimate a mating call?

My daily profession requires that I listen silently to people who tell me their various symptoms, their sadnesses and their ecstasies, and seldom have the noises of the avenue interfered. But the very civil servants of our wise fathers outdo the usual drivers when they scream their authoritative motorized battle cries at us peaceful citizens. Sometimes the culprits are the fire brigade, sometimes the police sirens welcoming a foreign celebrity. Here is an example of what can happen. One block away from me a playing little boy had satisfied his curiosity in his own technological way. He had carefully tested a fire alarm, not realizing, of course, that five minutes later a host of the most shrill and piercing sounds would be unleashed on him and the bystanders as the fire engines careened through the crowded streets. The scene becomes like a primitive tribe fighting magic danger with the most excruciating noises. By the time the fire chief arrives to inspect the situation, the nerve-racking work has already been accomplished. But more is to come, for hard upon the first feast of noises comes the higher pitched siren of the police car. – But presently quiet once more descends, leaving clear the way for the next hellish attack on our eardrums. Only then can I come down again to the dreams of my patients.

Every time I hear the fire monsters coming along the avenue with their siren songs, I am reminded of the German planes flying over alerted, war-torn London, and my inner alarm system is once more mobilized against the danger of death. My intuitive statistics tell me that at least twice a day I am reminded by the red monsters of the fire brigade that the ghosts of war and aggression are not dead in this metropolis.

Yet the noisy symphony of the city air is not finished with those cacophonic battle cries. The most penetrating and rasping attacks on our eardrums are launched by the official repair men, who with their pneumatic drills bore holes in the street in order to disappear deep in the rocky intestinal caves of our metropolis. This particular pandemonium of motorized hammer and axe – that racket of trembling and throbbing and burring – rattatats its way into cement and black rock below and produces the most deafening and earsplitting sound imaginable. It not only bores and penetrates and paralyzes one's eardrums, it drills itself much deeper into our very inner brain. During the First World War soldiers grew mad from the continual barrage on their eardrums. These pneumatic drills, it seems, are used by preference during the stillness of meditative weekends – for traffic reasons, I suppose.

Beyond this, the city has another silence-dispelling and noise making device. Every morning I am awakened by the crunching and grinding and whining undertone of the very useful sanitation truck. At this point I turn on my radio in order to offset one noise with a counter-noise, just as soldiers shoot their rifles to soothe themselves. Yet never in those ritualistic actions to evade the city's attack on my deepest auditive sensitivities have the tooting horns of cars played an important role for me. Why, I actually liked them! They reminded me of an orchestra whose leader was introducing a new set of tones for the instruments. I realized, of course, that a few perverse drivers were too aggressive with their horns. But their music was never so disturbing as the droning and barking of a heavy passing truck whose vibrations caused the very walls to tremble. I could not comprehend why the horns were so suddenly and so vehemently forbidden. This must be part of the great strategic battle against the motorized vehicle, against all those overpowered autocars which, in order to keep the wheels of industry turning, must be bought by the public in increasing quantities. Indeed, there exists a growing autocar compulsion, a technological conspiracy to motorize the citizen against his will and basic needs. Why else the colorful, alluring ads with which the auto magnates fill our periodicals? City fathers, if this battle of yours goes on, you will win my approval and have my vote. According to recent city ordinances, these everincreasing demons of speed are not supposed to be parked or even exist at all. Is the city fighting the car with its technological noises as a screen and tactical device, because it is unable to solve this battle between persuasive auto salesmanship on the one hand, and entirely inadequate parking space on the other? What have the noble city fathers to say in regard to those seductive car ads filling our newspapers and T.V. screens contrasted with the all too evident lack of garage and parking facilities?

On the other hand would not those city fathers – so interested in our quiet and mental wellbeing – become more forgiving if they realized the proud joy of sounding one's horn? The honk vies with the wink, the intimate friendly wink at a pretty girl.

Don't the authorities realize that the driver does not toot with his horn only to warn his external enemies, the pedestrians, but he also toots to get rid of his hostility and fears? Tooting is a magic act, dear coucilman. We need it in the nervous hunt of life. Our modern world makes more and more noises in order to get rid of its fears.

And why this relentless need to punish us with fines and tickets? How explain the furor of the noisy sirenblowing cops? Are New Yorkers only animals to be pursued and punished? Do the authorities really think to make the unhappy drivers better and more peaceful citizens by this method? Indeed the drivers have become the hunted ones, unprotected by their sounding horns, anchorless escapists for ticket-giving cops. Daily we are urged to dig down into our pockets in behalf of the god of speed, by buying bigger and faster cars, the use of which will end in either a car accident or the long, boring wait at the traffic court. How long is this rat race to go on?

Punishment is the worst way to educate a people into peaceful cooperation, at least that is what psychologists say on the problem. You city fathers arouse only rebellion and indifference. The police ticket replaces the so-needed order and regulation of a tremendous problem. Why don't you ask your cops to sound a punishing and warning siren scream into every over-tooting car? That would help much more to make the driver a silent, meditative philosopher.

Noisology – the mental hygiene of noise is a complicated science. According to my daily observation of the difficulty of obtaining a more peaceful atmosphere for my eardrums, the city government itself is even more guilty than others of causing disturbing noises, which outdo the constant cacophonia of all the honking drivers.

To honk or not to honk, to park or not to park, to punish or not to punish. These are the big questions involved in the ticket-distributing authorities. My neighbor's blaring radio can often be more distracting and sickening than any street noise, for I feel it as more personal and too close at hand. An urban quiet that vies with that of the countryside requires every noise-conditioned city dweller to make a new adjustment. Complete silence can pall, can haunt, and can even fill us with horror and anxiety.

It is no joke to contemplate this technological world of ours which is under constant auditory attack. For hygienists and psychologists it is still a problem what all those noises are doing to our minds. Part of the barrage has to be perceived and absorbed and stowed away in our minds. True, our mind learns to select, but in the midst of a plethora of noises – of radio, claxons, TV and nerve-shattering engines and human racket – our function of noise discrimination becomes more and more endangered. Some part of the din slips through the barriers of our mind and affects us more deeply.

Moments of quiet thought and meditation are increasingly difficult to find in our technological age. Inspiration and dreaming can no longer capture a yearned-for noiseless moment in which to relieve ourselves of the constant barrage. Nowhere may our eardrums rest from assault upon them.

No, my dear reader, this is not a complaint. I love the symphonic cacophony of street noises as much as you do. It somehow soothes my nerves. In the all-too-quiet hours, the dogs of my unconscious begin to bark and that is why I hum with you the music of our technological age. The purring and tooting of engines give us such a tremendous feeling of power and the loud noise I make compels the other fellow to listen. O paradox of silence!

For the peace of my private eardrums, I propose to the city fathers a few changes that might help us in our noise filled, overstimulated city life. A perpetual snow-carpet ten inches deep would be a help. The sudden silence of the town during the recent heavy snowfalls was truly wonderful. – though, as I said before, filling me with apprehension. Eventually we could order the big three of Detroit to stop, for a year or so, their advertising and seducing us into buying superfluous cars. We might also suggest that they invent horns and claxons producing a more Mozartian effect. Too, the cars could preferably be made without those mishandled crunching clutches. The torturing grinders and choppers of the sanitation department trucks, and the pneumatic drills of the street borers could even be muffled or enclosed in a soundproof chamber; and to humanize the whole situation the city policemen could be given some 'psychoanalytic' training, which would lead them to hold kind and human conversations with offenders in order to seek the spontaneous cooperation of the public – rather than resort to the enervating punishing ticket books!

And last but not least, let us ask the fire department to regress – to swing back to their old harmonious jingle of bells to announce that they require the right of way. Why was this quaint but more humane outfit ever scrapped?

How sweet will our future sleep and quiet be – if we can tolerate it!

15.   Mental Contagion and Emotional Infection *

In unfolding his timebinding principle Korzybski explained that this principle is essentially the reason why each new generation has the opportunity to begin where the older generation leaves off. History and time are condensed in various ways. We find this condensation in the chemical structure of the genes, the so-called carriers of heredity in which the history of biological adaptation and learning is conserved, while words, symbols, myths and traditions are endowed with the evolution of man's subjective experiences and deducted abstractions.

Where does a speaker begin? Where, in the vast conglomerate of inner and outer experiences, lies the subject of this essay?

My first encounter with the science of semantics and verbal meaning – which in its beginning was called 'significs' – took place in my native Holland some forty years ago, when I was a medical student. The movement in the Low Lands started when in 1897 the Dutch physician and author, Frederik Van Eeden, published his study on 'The Logical Basis of Mutual Relations'.[5] Though he founded his work on the well known pioneering investigations of Bréal[3] and Lady Welby[18], he went his own way and formulated, already then, some semantic questions about official thinking which he called quasi-scientific abstractions and quasi-logic automatisms.

How surprised I was to find a flourishing science of general

* Alfred Korzybski Memorial Lecture for the Institute of General Semantics, New York, April 28, 1964.

semantics and psycholinguistics, going far beyond our limited venture, when I settled in this country after the Second World War. Yet, tonight I am not going to rephrase my personal and limited understanding of that vast edifice founded by Korzybski and his students. My subject is mental contagion and emotional infection. What do I mean with that label? You will not find these words in the textbooks on psychology, sociology, or psychiatry. Nevertheless, the concept is used in everyday vernacular. The newspapers write about ideological contamination or political infection, about epidemie criminality and the spreading of pathological habits. Psychologists speak about suggestion and the more inadvertent induction of behavior. The infectious dissemination of violence is at this moment a special point of order. Psychiatrists mention infectious psychoses or the unconscious transfer of feelings, thoughts, and actions. Korzybski, in his introduction to 'Science and Sanity', writes about the concept of infectious identification.[7]

All this is reason enough to look more closely at this subject of mental contagion or psychic contamination. Be aware that all these words are borrowed from the science of infectious diseases. Accordingly, we will unwittingly look for communicable units, for psychic germs going from one person to the other. Although the concept of mental contagion is still undefined, all the metaphors, used up till now point at a hidden and inadvertent transfer of feeling, thinking, and action.

But before we start to look at the clinical facts I have to come back to an unanswered question: Where does all this fit into the science of general semantics, founded by the man in whose honor we have gathered here tonight? I have to go back to Spinoza who in his herkological approach of 'omne determinatio est negatio' taught us that in order to learn to explore and define we have to be well aware of our limitations, that is to say to be aware how bound we are by our suppositions and by our tools of research. We first have to walk around our subject in order to determine what distorts and inhibits our outlook. Like in a bowling game, we attempt many throws at our subject of observation hoping to hit the core of the problem in the end.

Let us tentatively accept that mental contagion intrudes into our feeling and thinking unobtrusively. Mental contagion comprises, as it were, the science of concealed communication of all that intrudes into our clear semantic thinking and troubles the higher abstractions. I want to show that such psychic infection takes away the consciousness of abstracting and that it pushes us unwittingly back to a non-verbal level of relating. Just like minute neurophysiological occurrences – as for instance a small stroke – can change our ability to conceptualize, so are our verbal rationalizations and abstractions distorted by inadvertent environmental attitudes and suggestions. Indeed, we speak of infectious psychological climates. Mental contagion dulls the awareness of the fact that we must continually go over and above the doctrinal compliance asked for by our environment and especially by our colleagues. It coerces and distorts our endeavor to think clearly and it robs our mental apparatus from its highest aim, namely, to think in an unbiased way. An information technician would say that we have to be on guard at all times for disturbing noises in our communication system. Mental contagion in the form of unobtrusive brainwashing can be a permanent intruder into our critical and semantic endeavor and into our systems of orientation.

I now have to warn my readers that many people feel an unpleasant resistance against this subject. The idea that other people's emotions and thoughts can unexpectedly intrude into our thinking affects our illusion of psychic autonomy. We want to ward off such eerie concepts. Yet, when I go deeper into this subject the reader will become more familiar with what I have to relate. Remember that those who have become more acquainted with the concept of mental contagion are inadvertently starting to build defenses against this unobtrusive influence and are thus able to better eliminate self-deception. It is the same with myths: those who accept myths for what they are will no longer be lured by them.

Allen Walker Read[14] gives a beautiful example of disturbing aggressive noises from Civil War days in this country. He tells us how the unexpected 'rebel-yell' of the Confederates completely demoralized the Yankees until they familiarized themselves with this weapon of psychological warfare. Yelling, of course, better not be part of a meeting to which scientists came in order to discuss philosophical and psychological subjects. But every lecture is a symbolic fight in which we mutually probe: Who has the strongest psychic impact? I want my ideas to measure themselves with yours. Instead of yelling, or fencing with steel, I use word symbols. Those symbols, traveling between listener or reader and me, are loaded with manifold meanings which everybody interprets in his own personal way, grasping parts of the semantic and emotional intention behind my sophisticated symbols and my gestural actions. Various additional little cues in my communication will decide whether my readers are going to accept or reject my presentation.

Let us now look at the clinical considerations to see if some general rules of mental contagion can be established.

THE PATTERN OF INTERACTION OR MAN'S HORIZONTAL PSYCHIC CONDITIONING

Man exists through personal interaction. This is true even for a hermit who, in his own mind, lives at the center of a network of relationships. We know relatively little about this web of cross-relations that is continually active. It has been known for some time that a case of panic in one individual can instantaneously induce collective panic in a group of people, and hysterical behavior on the part of one person will spread like wildfire and easily affects an entire crowd. There are numerous examples of such psychological chainreactions. It is also true that some people are immune and keep their distance, usually because they are better aware of the interaction between them and the group. On the whole we find that little systematic attention has been devoted to the concepts of mutual interaction, of positive or negative influences, or other forms of behavioral contamination. Psychiatric literature has produced numerous examples of *psychoses à deux* or *psychoses à trois*, and of infectious psychoses[16] within families or in small communities. Diagnostically one has to detect the pathogenic nucleus inside the group. Mob psychology is for a great part the science of the psychic germ carriers. There are also several cases known where a latent psychotic parent pushes the child into abnormal or even criminal behavior. The child acts out, as it were, what the parent represses in himself although the elder is often quick enough to punish the youngster for his asocial behavior. The so-called *school phobia* is thought to be most probably motivated by the mother's unconscious separation anxiety: she does not want the child to leave her.

By and large the theme of human interaction has been receiving more attention since through psychotherapy greater emphasis has been placed on therapeutic human encounter and the interrelation between patient and therapist. Moreover, the subtle parent-child relationship with its symbiotic beginnings is now looked upon as the initial conditioner of the molding pattern of man's psychic functions. Families live together happily or tensely, depending on the example set by the parents and their guidance. Omission as well as commission condition the child. In every group a specific climate of mutual interaction is established and its quality usually depends on the leaders. From practical experience in the classroom we are aware that teachers are able to influence not only the morale of the entire class but also the mutual relationships between the students. Often the pattern of interaction is set at the beginning of the school year. A teacher unwittingly influences his class through his mood, be it good or bad, while by the same principle a student with a nervous tic can infect his fellow pupils.

Books on human ecology or social psychology rarely touch upon the facts of mental contagion. Yet everyone is daily subjected to a multitude of influences that somehow fashion and alter his habits. It is a continuous bombardment by influences, with micro-conditionings and tiny seductions. Apart from the presence of atomic particles in the air that can gradually and insidiously change man's biologic condition, there are manifold subtle psychological conditioning units that bring about changes in people, in their interactions and their environment. The little noxious pinpricks and insinuations of life are often more traumatic than the great shocks.

Man is not a separate individual who can preserve his independence. He is the nucleus of a social unit upon which language, history, tradition, myth, personal genesis and group influences are continually hammering away. This fact of daily interaction and coercion, which is the subject of every study of human communication, hurts man's illusions of having an independent ego – so much so that he is inclined to resist taking this vulnerability into account. Whenever two people meet, the stronger personality, after an initial period of psychic probing, knowingly or otherwise tries to coerce the weaker one, attempting to become the leader. Several patterns of interaction in which psychic contagion plays an important role can be detected. Between harmonious sharing together and the ultimate of permanent one-sided dominance lies a gamut of variations.

Man's personal and historical past may be called the *vertical* molding influences, his social environment the *horizontal* conditioner, as suggested by Ehrenwald in his studies on neurotic interaction in the family.[6]

EACH MAN IS A CROWD

It may come as a shock to some that man is not a distinctly set off entity with a constant self but rather the focal point of a field of influences, and the nucleus of various passive disseminations and active participations in community life. Each man plays several social roles. He is *not* the sum total of what he *consciously* experiences. There is a vast reservoir of subliminal experiences and a large pyramid of unconscious and biological drives impelling his actions. He is not only that separate unique human being that his reflection in the mirror shows him to be; he is not only that highly original creative thinker the poet sings of. He borrows more than he knows from his epoch and the *Zeitgeist*, he absorbs continually from history and tradition, and as an individual creator he soaks up as much as he can to mold and transform into some kind of personal *Gestalt*. Collectively, the listeners have also a share in the composition of music as the composer himself as long as the audiences create and recreate the accumulated harmonies in the inner ear of their listening minds. A Mozart born in the twentieth century might have turned out a different kind of music. To be sure, creative geniuses do transform the world in which they live; Hadley Cantril calls them the goal-directed transactions that go beyond the mere interactions.[4] There are also the talented molders, as well as the mere plagiarists, and don't forget that the very word we speak is a form of plagiarism. Politicians, so utterly dependent on competitive election-strategy and public approval are even more products of the *Zeitgeist* and are continually being shaped and conditioned by the mass emotions of their electorates.

In our world of today there are very few moral authorities and individuals who have transcended the overwhelming network of influences and dare to be unique and wise personalities. The cacophony of noises tends to drown the voices of wisdom. Telephone, radio and television bring daily hypnosis into our living room. Television violence disseminates a contagious and perverting influence on to our youths. Horror does not pacify but nearly always, exacerbates hidden rage in each of us. Whereas executive power and dictatorship admittedly exist in our world, there is virtually no affirmation of the wisdom of a single unique human being.

When my book on brainwashing, thought control and menticide[12] first came out in 1956, several critics assumed that I was describing an extreme political phenomenon characteristic only of totalitarian regimes. The fact is that a major part of the book is dedicated to the non-obtrusive, quiet persuasion of minds that takes place in all personal encounters in every civilization. I pointed out how institutionalization and technicalization of our community life unobtrusively changes people's attitudes into automatic conformity and obedience, while simultaneously affecting their approach to personal responsibilities and commitments.

Descartes' *Cogito ergo sum* (I think, therefore I am) needs revising for our times: I think, therefore I re-think other people's thoughts. I think, therefore I borrow from history and plagiarize my teachers' ideas. I think, therefore I am influenced and concentrate on thoughts inadvertently put into my head by other people's utterances and by the daily headlines. I think, therefore I reshape other people's ideas. This new position of man in the technical age demands great modesty about any direct personal impact on history.

In our affluent society a paradoxical phenomenon exists in advertising and in the machinery that engineers public opinion. In order to justify their existence, these institutions have to tax their ingenuity to the utmost so as to create *artificial dissatisfaction in a relatively satisfied economy*. It is a culture aimed at achieving thoroughly saturated gratification, with people continually on the lookout for newer and more thrilling needs, 'guided' by an artificial creation of new wants, combined with empty ways of filling leisure time. Because of more leisure time, our society is perhaps more prone to mass suggestion than a culture in which primary human needs have not yet been fulfilled. Boredom provides a fertile soil for the seeds of suggestibility. Boredom can even have a luring hypnotic effect and can be more persuasive for some people than the clarity of purposeful work. Indeed, there exist delights of boredom but the results of boredom are often disastrous. Human aggression, competition and even destruction may be aroused and unleashed, although minds at leisure can be kept occupied and turned away from the great void of senseless living. As we have noted elsewhere[13], it is all too true that regressive bestial feelings are more easily invoked and spread by propaganda than noble ones, according to the rules of mental contagion, some of which I now have to explain.

DIRECT MENTAL INDUCTION AND REGRESSION TO ARCHAIC COMMUNICATION

As we already heard, various synonyms are used to designate the phenomenon of mental contagion. We are all 'moved' by other people's emotions. Sometimes this emotional transfer is spoken of as moral contagion, sometimes as infectious defamation or contagious placing of blame. Stimulating propaganda is often called inflammatory. Again the referral to infectious diseases! A politician may speak of people being susceptible to other political currents because of their persuasive impact. One can refer to infestation with panic, or behavioral contamination, or the suggestive sloganization of a group.

Many a teacher complains of the one pupil who is having a bad influence on his class, officers report a few soldiers who have formed an infectious nucleus of panicky cowards in their companies. The psychiatrist describes infectious mass psychoses or, as mentioned before, smaller epidemics of *psychoses à deux* or *psychoses à trois*. He considers all these a special aspect of pathological intercommunication. In nonpathological cases he talks about contagious family interaction.

These subtle interactions are the products of the intricate web of communications that surrounds man. We live in a field of continuous intercommunication with conscious as well as subliminal perception. Stimuli from within and from outside, of which we are more or less aware, reach us continually. Even while asleep we are not completely cut off from sensory contact with our environment. Experiments show that under anesthesia the cerebral cortex registers sensory stimuli even more vehemently, though no awareness or reactive response follows. Exploration of the psychotherapeutic process has brought to light the existence of unconscious pre-verbal communication as well as unobtrusive subliminal information, both making use of infinitesimal verbal and gestural clues, and also of extrasensory perception. There is rhythmic induction and interaction, gesture and sound, and, at the very summit of mutual verbal contact the various levels of semantic exchange. In this essay attention will be given to the immediate induction and transfer caused by various forms of archaic communication.

Archaic communication exists of the innate bodily signals and the adaptational responses existing before and immediately after birth.

The social intercourse established by innate bodily signal codes held in common by man and beast form part and parcel of

185

archaic communication. Everyone understands and reacts to the distress calls of animals. Certain emotional expressions are immediately understood. Crying, laughing, rhythmic tapping, yawning, fright reactions, fainting, itching, dancing movements, sneezing, shouting, convulsions, erotic gestures – they all invoke immediate understanding and response. If I would imitate with my hands the movement of yawning without warning you, many in my audience would be inwardly forced to take over the sign and begin to yawn. Nothing is more contagious than a yawn – a sign of boredom – or the rhythmically reiterated shout of a crowd – the Nazi '*Sieg Heil, Sieg Heil*', or the fascist '*Duce, Duce, Duce*'. If such primary expressions are not checked by self-restraint and dignified behavior, mental contagion is all the more apt to take hold.

Throughout history there have been numerous infectious dance epidemics. On a note of levity one might mention 'Rock 'n' Roll', the 'Twist', and more recently the 'Beatle' craze. Rhythm in one person provokes rhythm in others. It is important to note that direct mental induction through rhythm and psychic co-oscillation follow a definite rule. *The more an emotional expression reflects regression to the archaic biological sign code, the more contagious that expression will be.* A yawning child, for instance, affects all the other children in the class. Somebody who is scratching causes others to feel itchy. Mental contagion means, in this instance, a common unobtrusive regression to a more primitive, pre-verbal sign language and biological code directly understood by all. The primordial units of mental infection are those in history and time acquired adaptational responses that have a universal appeal. The biological and symbolic *timebinders* bind us to identical responses. In medicine we speak of communicable diseases caused by infectious units. Similarly in psychology can we refer to primordial transferable units of behavior which compel fellow beings to co-oscillate as it were and to react similarly or in the opposite way. These inductions coming from outside our individual realm intrude into our clear semantic thinking and by their emotional impact hamper the life of reason. Mental contagion is related to man's deep symbiotic needs and his utter dependency. More than any other animal he is dependent on the guidance of his fellows. It is as if the rising gap between maturing humans has to be bridged by various new methods of inter-communication. The biological basis of communication establishes the direct empathy that predominates in the mother-child relation and lives forth in all of us in the process of direct identification. Lately psychiatry studied more extensively the permanent symbiotic ties that can remain between individuals and is most probably one of the tenets of telepathy. As the distance between mother and child grows an urgent need for other more symbolic avenues of communication becomes established. Thus in every group-relation where the old symbiotic tie from early childhood is re-enacted – e.g. in societies where individualization is not emphasized, sometimes not even tolerated – the facts of mental contagion become more apparent. Social rites and symbols make their specific psychic demands on the individual. Even the outsider is affected, though it may be in a negative way. The group frequently induces the stranger's opposition and his negativistic warding off of psychic entanglement. It has been observed that mental infection increases when established social institutions collapse and the group regresses to more primitive means of intercommunication. Regression can also be the result of the shock of not understanding and lack of comprehension in a world that outgrows its traditions too rapidly. Reactive stupidity and the forsaking of intelligent endeavor often follow social revolutions.

When the individual's ego boundaries and ego defenses are weakened as the result of exhaustion or disease – which in semantic terms means that he has to abandon his high levels of reason and abstraction – he is more easily suggestible and invariably feels himself to be a more passive victim of outside stimuli. This process can go so far that people feel completely defenseless. In *schizophrenic doxasm* we find the patient suffering from delusions of relatedness in which he feels as if his mind and brain were laid bare to every evil intention of others – a condition which he also interprets as being brainwashed or victimized by mysterious rays.

However, man's involuntary regression under the burden of group action and mental contagion is not *always* a negative phenomenon. Unfavorable forms of regression do exist, leading to loss of self, to primitivity, chaos and decay. But there is a positive side of regression leading to revitalization and towards new adaptations of the individual organism. We must bear this ambivalence in mind. In sleep and in our dreams we all regress and at the same time regenerate our inner forces. Sleep, as Shakespeare says, knits up 'the ravelled sleeve of care'. While the group, with its greater chance of mutual contamination tends to incite the individual to regress to primitive actions, its continuity and its protective influence can prevent the individual from regressing too much. Tradition and social ritual, however rigid they may be, have a way of bracing the mental backbone of those who have not yet developed a well rounded self-awareness.

The old mystics believed in a collective emotional state with which the logic of thought only interfered. In other words people participate in the same feelings, but when it comes to the conceptualization of thought and the distantiation required by word and concept they are apt to diverge. I am thinking here specifically of the classroom, this most common experimental group. Thought, reflection and discussion slowly make individual entities of the participants, although they never gain complete independence from the thoughts of their teachers. For this they need the verification of varied thoughts of different instructors who teach them to look at a subject from different angles.

The ambivalent relation between group and indioidual is clearly demonstrated by man's motivation for mutual participation and symbiotic enjoyment. The group comes together not only for mutual collaboration and friendly cooperation, but also with a hostile intention of which it is less aware, namely to exclude others, to let off steam and to ban and sometimes persecute the black sheep and the scapegoats who have to be offered to the gods of hatred and revenge. This inadvertent urge to vent common hidden aggression on outsiders is one of the fundamentals of group prejudice. Scapegoatism and prejudice rear their heads early, first within the family, then in the classroom. Racial prejudice is in many ways a displacement and a compounding of earlier sibling rivalry. The semantics of prejudice and vituperation teach us again how infectious rage and hatred can be.

Increased inner tension may lead groups to burden themselves with an enormous load of rules and regulations, and with extreme legal restrictions as a protection against inner ambivalence and conflict. We see another solution of these internal antinomies, for instance, in totalitarian regimes. The greater their internal trouble the more intense will be their search for outside enemies and scapegoats. Demagogic strategy also employs psychic contamination, whereby resentment is used as a common arouser of aggression.

By contrast, a democracy founded on freedom wants to impose a minimum of law, asking of the individual a greater measure of humanism, dignity and self-control than the law requires. The essential difference between enforced dictatorial legalism and the freedom of voluntary personal commitment lies in the confidence men have in their intentions toward each other. This self-confidence is stimulated by personal example and emotional transfer of mutual trust. One of the most important factors in learning and maturing is the wholesome example set by consistent, benevolent and wise leadership. This is what we might call the converse form of mental contagion through good and just examples.

MAN'S VERTICAL CONDITIONING

The fact that man's feeling and thinking are not only influenced by the present but are also products of long historical vertical tradition comes to the fore particularly at times when he feels threatened in his social and private existence. Throughout the world, whenever conquerors and tyrannical occupiers have tried to change the social and economical relations in a country, a resurgence of historical interest has always been the result. In my native Holland, after the Nazi occupation, books on historical topics were at the top of the bestseller lists. We can regard this revival of interest partly as a form of escape into the days of yore, into the glory and heroism of the past. However, it is more than escape because history and tradition are the mental roots which gave life to the very group that is now in danger.

There is no doubt that this *identification with the past* and pride in heritage can be inspiring and may give birth to the most vital ideas and energies a group or a nation possesses. We carry within us not only a feeling of *horizontal* identity, of doing what the Jones's and the Smith's are doing, but also a *vertical* or historical identity. This is what justifies our painstaking teaching of history in the schoolroom. Yet this same vertical identification may result in the most primitive regression to antiquated myths and black magic, such as the world experienced in Nazi mythology with its glorification of the blond beast in man and the ancient Germanic need for doom and Nemesis. Our illusion of fast progress and change fails to give sufficient attention to these history and time bound patterns behind the façades of modernism.

The words man speaks have their roots in a history of different meanings. These meanings unconsciously reverberate in the word-symbols with which he expresses himself. Symbols are indeed the genes of history. Linguists have aptly described how our thinking is fashioned by the treasure of verbal tools at our disposal. Our thinking is tied up with our language, and to close the circle, because of the language we use we are unwittingly bound up with the historical modes of thinking that language represents[15]. In turn, the language handed down to us directs our modes of perception.[17]

Another example of vertical conditioning of our behavior is what we might call pseudo-heredity – the subtle interaction from generation to generation. Without denying the facts of biological heredity, Ehrenwald[6] gave a crystal clear description how generations of obsessive-compulsive people (the Obscomp family) laid the groundwork of the same conditioning milieu for the next generation, so that the same old pattern of pathological psychic defenses had to be built up again by the newcomers.

Developmental psychology has only begun to delve into the many psychic interrelations and interactions that exist between generations. In a paper on the influence of television and other means of communication on family interaction, I demonstrated how degenerating and apathizing the growing lack of emotional contact between the generations can be, especially since our technical know how makes it easier for them to justify individual aloofness. Withdrawn parents make for either rebellious children or for withdrawn ones. In a mechanized society, steeped in what amounts to an automatic urge to conform, the youngster's hostility and even his delinquency can be one of the paradoxical protests against the feeling of annihilation of his individual dignity. Numerous clinical examples exist of a form of passive destructive robotism that follows every command issued, be it criminal or otherwise. Eichmann was the very example of such a robot full of conscientiousness, yet without a conscience. Technical automatization gives people the impression of a restless going on, a speedomania that prevents thinking and precludes the awareness that many precious things exist beyond and even contrary to mere doing. The age of haste threatens to destroy our capacity for individual meditation.

Specific sensitive phases exist in the development of the individual in which traumatic occurrences may have a deep conditioning impact making people more vulnerable to mental contagion during that period. There are, for instance, ultra sensitive developmental periods, such as the walking crisis of the infant and the Weltschmerz years of adolescence which can render the growing individual temporarily more vulnerable to stressful impact and to greater molding from outside. Every educator has to be mindful of this fluctuation of formative impact by the environment. Going to school, a first token separation from the mother, is one such reconditioning phase in the life of the child. With the help of the teacher the child can either start a pattern of corrected sibling rivalry by improving relationships with his peers, or its old separation phobias can become aggravated.

A cornerstone in the study of mental contagion is the clinical acceptance of historical causation in the individual development of human behavior. We accept the fact that a repressed, highly traumatic experience from the past can be reactivated when a recent dramatic occurrence suddenly triggers off the old despair which might otherwise have left no traces and been forgotten forever. Victims who passed their adolescent years in concentration camps live constantly on such a precarious mental tightrope. Every new stressful emotion triggers off desperate feelings connected with the past and these powerful feelings threaten to send their victims hurtling to the ground.

HORIZONTAL SOCIAL CONDITIONING

Which are the horizontal factors that contribute to mental contagion? When considering ecological and psychological factors that condition and direct human behavior we generally think in terms of conscious persuasion, or more forcefully, mental coercion. Yet there are many unobtrusive influences in society which shape our lives, often with as great an impact. For example technicalization and institutionalization – more than other cultural phenomena – have destroyed many a person's belief in himself as a self-governing individual. He feels caught up in a network of suggestions difficult for him to offset with his private opinion and his own ethical evaluation because he is usually not aware that these suggestions exist. We must distinguish here between *depersonification* – a temporary defensive surrender of the individual's integrity to mass influences, which is a universal and normal process – and *depersonalization*, which is a process of psychotic breakdown of the ego.

In the German S.S. state every soldier had to be an automatic, obedient follower. His oath of loyalty implied complete and unquestioning obedience to the orders from his Führer and was absolutely binding. Were he to become morally conscious and critical of the commands he had to follow, his only moral choice would be flight or suicide. The loyalty oath, an old magic tool of mental contagion instituted to ensnare man's conscience in a sand trap of unceasing loyalty, is still one of the great illusionary equalizers of our time. The fact is that mature man cannot be unconditionally submissive to a fallible fellow man. He needs real terror or terrorizing fantasies to incite him to submit. Dictatorial coercion enforced by terror changes nearly every one into an automatic submissive conformist. Even the onlooker who wants to steer clear of this process is not immune to the gradual equalization of minds through his inadvertent interaction and sympathy with other people's fears and sorrows.

Time does not permit a description of all the intricacies of unconscious and unobtrusive mental coercion. Suffice it to say that we have become increasingly aware that systematic masspersuasion, mass-suggestion, and mental mass-coercion do exist. Every group, every society, and every culture exert stresses and tensions which have a molding and conditioning impact on its members. In the *Saturday Review* of September 6, 1958, the late Senator Richard L. Neuberger described a panicky surrender of the U.S. Senate to a highly charged emotional collective confusion. The subject under debate was whether to vote funds for a study on 'Strategic Surrender'. Few had taken the trouble to read the volume in question but the key word 'surrender' had aroused a feverish excitement that finally led the Senators to surrender to collective emotions of pseudo-heroism rather than weighing with reason the matter under scrutiny. Indeed, mental contagion is related to the bolstering of hidden anxieties and our defenses against them.

Studies by Benedict[2] and Mead[3] show how special traditional habits determine the aspect of a culture from the very onset. We speak, for instance, of schizogenic societies (Bali) and paranoiogenic societies (the Dobu and the Nazis). Also, we refer to apathizing and criminogenic societies, or to shame-and-guilt societies. It is all dependent on how conditioned and internalized the various individual and social responsibilities in these cultures have become. A society usually hands its members, in addition to the verbiage and labels, a cluster of articulations, justifications, and cliché's, giving the reasons why the participants are expected to adjust to that society's code, prejudices, and ceremonials. This 'platform' usually tends to obscure the fact of need for compliance and psychological submission. Because politicians always have to manipulate the instrument of persuasion, they themselves are often victimized by their own tool and become more vulnerable to suggestion. The same is true of hypnotists.

Man's innate masochism rooted in his need for dependency plays an important role in his nearly automatic submission to doctrines. To give a paradoxical example, social tension and stress as such do not always have a direct anxiety provoking impact on man. Sometimes it is the cessation of tension, the liberation from burdens, and the frustration caused by sudden unprepared-for leisure that cannot be creatively filled, that affect man's equilibrium. Panic, for instance, can develop when danger and stress are over, precisely because the tense misery has passed. Many people do not know what to do with their pre-ordained defensive · attitudes once outside dangers are eliminated. To translate this into educational terms we can say that the absence of rules and the lack of discipline in a broken or weakened family can arouse all the panic of unchecked unconscious drives in a child. Education has to help the child discipline his crude instinctual impulses. No society can forego the need for restraint.

Social tension, coercion, and the compulsion to conformity better *fulfill* immature human needs when aligned with substitute gratifications such as utopian expectation, self-adulation, or externalized hatred as manifested in prejudice and scapegoatism. The contagion of aggression, excitement and debunking helps people to let off steam. Many people have an aversion to individual freedom because such freedom must lead to greater responsibility and individual commitment.

Man looks at the world not through rose-colored glasses but through the lenses of his biased emotions. The slave can be made to believe that he lives in paradise, while those who have the luxury of freedom and independence can be talked into suffering daily feelings of deprivation and dissatisfaction. Indeed, in our technical era the emptiness of more leisure time has become for many a new burden calling for new adaptations.

How man is influenced and mentally infected by his horizontal social conditioning can easily be demonstrated in the relatively small world of psychologists and psychiatrists. The *theoretical* schisms between these practitioners of the art of mental healing are usually determined by the school the student happened to visit and subsequently by his teacher's opinions rather than by his own initial verification of facts and thoughts. The student's initiation [into a specific psychological group or subgroup is more often directed by similar social and ecological factors – suggestion, economic wherewithal, and prejudice – than by elaborate study of the various pros and cons of his adopted psychological system and its competing views.

Man's freedom starts by delineating his unfreedom. That is why we have to study the spiderweb of communication that invades our freedom of thinking and abstracting, We cannot merely study man as a concrete, independent, self-enclosed entity. He always lives in a field of multifarious influences. Even as a scientist he remains a benign plagiarist, and this is true of the philosopher as well. The words we speak are taken over from the language of thousands of generations. Although we impute to each other a similar manner of thinking and feeling, it is because of our disparate backgrounds that we all give a different interpretation to the words we hear.

Nevertheless, man is in continuous mutual relation and communication. Again, the loneliest hermit carries within his mind his fantasied companions with whom he has inner conversations. Everyone is in himself a center of psychic reception and absorption. Man is also a transmitter of messages. There is no such thing as an isolated self – one is primarily a group of shifting ego-boundaries in continual exchange with the ego-boundaries of others.

In communicating, the core of the other person is rarely reached. The much talked-about I or Ego or Self, residing within its boundaries, is a hypothetical central pilot who receives as well as broadcasts messages. He relays the incoming communications according to an inherited and acquired code and, in addition, he may be a thinker for himself and a doer in his own right. These central pilots are agents acting upon various influences according to their innate sense and the code imprinted on or developed within them.

Man's need for an elaborate network of communication is related to the absence of ripe instincts at birth. His foetalization, biological retardation, and his lack of agile adaptation cause him among all animals to be almost completely dependent on his parents and peers during infancy and early childhood. By opposing his peers, man remains related to them. Within the intricate communication network he perpetually classifies himself as to where he belongs, where he wants to be accepted, what network he fits into or wishes to fit into.

Man's self-realization implies his being aware of his continual interdependence and interrelation even in his maturity. With Plato we may say that reason makes people less amenable to coercion. A strong *feeling* of self usually betrays a satisfactory social adaptation – one feels accepted and successful. It does not always mean *being* a strong autarchic ego. Many subtle clues are used in this never-ending process of social selection and verification whereby various people are included or excluded from the individual crowd we call the total person.

SUMMARY

Mental contagion delineates the science of concealed communication, of the manifold hidden clues and disturbing noises in the system of mutual information. The study of psychic infection shows, more than the individual analysis of man, how intimately bound up man's emotions and behavior are with his environment and his biological and historical past. Both biological and historical time are condensed in man and determine his limitations. This brief survey of the influence of mental contagion in personal and social interaction shows first that man is an individual crowd, a complex being directed by manifold internalized suggestions and identifications through which traditions, parents, family habits, and teachers unobtrusively shape him. Man is not only an individual thinker but his cultural traditions and the *Zeitgeist* think *in* him and *for* him through an intricate web of communications. We are brainwashed as it were by our own, and our fellow beings' primitivisms.

Vertical mental contagion is the product of the influence of linguistic conditioning, of history, tradition and pseudo-heredity through interaction of generations. Horizontal mental contagion is the result of the unobtrusive mental exchange, persuasion and coercion that condition man's behavior. Simple rules can be formulated for the contagiousness of psychic phenomena. The more a human expression resembles an archaic and innate biological adaptation the more it forces fellow beings to react in the same way. Cooscillation with and induction by archaic communication is the core of mental contagion.

The unique individuality in the 'internalized crowd' gets a greater chance to assert itself when critical assessment of existing persuasions and suggestions can be made and the person can distantiate himself from the web of conscious and inadvertent communications that are molding him. We may finish with Spinoza's adagium that 'man's freedom starts by delineating his unfreedom'.

BIBLIOGRAPHY

1. BARBU, Z., *Problems of Historical Psychology*. New York, Grove Press, 1960.
2. BENEDICT, R., *Patterns of Culture*. New York, Houghton Mifflin, 1939.
3. BREAL, M., *Essai de Semantique*. Paris, Hachette, 1884.
4. CANTRIL, H., 'The Individual's Demand on Society' in *The Dilemma of Organizational Society*. New York, Dutton, 1963.
5. EEDEN, F. VAN, *Redekundige Grondslag Van Verstandhouding*. in *Studies*. Amsterdam, Versluys, 1897.
6. EHRENWALD, J., *Neurosis in the Family*. New York, Hoeber, 1963.
7. KORZYBSKI, A., *Science and Sanity*, The International Non-Aristotelian Library Publishing Company, Lakeville, Connecticut, 1958.
8. MEAD, M. and METRAUX, R., *The Study of Culture at a Distance*. U. of Chicago Press, 1959.
9. MEERLOO, J.A.M., *Conversation and Communication*. New York, Int. Universities Press, 1952.
10. MEERLOO, J.A.M., 'Mental Contagion.' *Am. J. Psychotherapy*, Vol. XIII, 1959, pp. 66-82.

11. MEERLOO, J.A.M., 'The Network of Communication.' *Am. J. Psychotherapy*, Vol. XIV, 1960.

12. MEERLOO, J.A.M., *The Rape of the Mind*. New York, World Publishing Company, 1956.

13. MEERLOO, J.A.M., 'The Dual Meaning of Reggression.' *Psychoanalytic Review*, Vol. 50, 1962.

14. READ, A.W., 'The Rebel Yell as a Linguistic Problem,' *American Speech*, Vol. 36, 1961.

15. SAPIR, E., *Selected Writings*. Berkeley, California University Press, 1949.

16. TOLSMA, F.J., 'Modern Psychiatric Views on the Induced Psychosis.' *Folia Psychiatrica Neerlandica*, Vol. 54, 1951.

17. WHORF, B.L., *Language, Thought and Reality*. New York, John Wiley and Sons, 1956.

18. WELBY, V., *Signifies and Language*. London, Macmillan, 1911.